Georgia Nature Weekends

Fifty-two Adventures in Nature

Terry Johnson

FALCON®

Guilford, Connecticut
An imprint of The Globe Pequot Press

The prices and rates listed in this guidebook were confirmed at press time. We recommend, however, that you call establishments before traveling to obtain current information.

A FALCON GUIDE ®

Copyright © 2002 by The Globe Pequot Press

Cover photos: Terry Johnson
Text design: Lisa Reneson
Map design: Trapper Badovinac
Photo credits: All photos by the author, except page 77 by Erica LeMoine and page 151 by Barb Zoodsma.

Library of Congress Cataloging-in-Publication Data
Johnson, Terry, 1944–
Georgia nature weekends: 52 adventures in nature / Terry Johnson. —1st ed.
   p. cm.
ISBN 0-7627-1101-9
   1. Natural history—Georgia—Guidebooks. 2. Wildlife watching—Georgia—Guidebooks. 3. Georgia—Guidebooks. I. Title.

QH105.G4 J64 2001
508.758—dc21   200104099

Manufactured in the United States of America
First Edition/First Printing

Georgia
Nature Weekends

Help Us Keep This Guide Up to Date

Every effort has been made by the author and editors to make this guide as accurate and useful as possible. However, many things can change after a guide is published—establishments close, phone numbers change, hiking trails are rerouted, facilities come under new management, etc.

We would love to hear from you concerning your experiences with this guide and how you feel it could be improved and kept up to date. While we may not be able to respond to all comments and suggestions, we'll take them to heart, and we'll also make certain to share them with the author. Please send your comments and suggestions to the following address:

The Globe Pequot Press
Reader Response/Editorial Department
P.O. Box 480
Guilford, CT 06437

Or you may e-mail us at:

editorial@globe-pequot.com

Thanks for your input, and happy travels!

Dedication

To Donna, Angela, and Anna

Contents

Summer

Winter

Acknowledgments

I am deeply indebted to many people for helping with this book. Without their unselfish assistance, this volume would not be possible.

I would be remiss if I didn't thank my mother, Mildred Johnson, for nurturing my love of writing. Looking back, I don't know how she was able to make me sit still long enough to learn to write with baseball, fishing, and the natural world demanding my attention.

I want to extend a special thank you to Don Pfitzer for having enough confidence in me to recommend me for this project. I also want to express my appreciation for the valuable advice he offered whenever questions regarding the development of the book arose.

I am especially grateful to Walter Leverett for his skillful preparation of the excellent maps that appear in this book. His painstaking attention to detail is remarkable.

I express my gratitude to Jerry and Rose Payne, the two best naturalists I have ever met. They always seemed to have the answer to any natural history question that I posed to them.

A special thanks to Michelle McLaunin for helping edit the text.

I also want to offer my thanks to Barb Zoodsma, Linda Guy, Season Platt, Mike Chapman, Don Cohrs, and Luann Craighton for generously offering information and assistance.

I express my gratitude to my daughter Angela for suggesting topics, visiting sites, and assisting with the revision.

Finally, I cannot begin to say how much I appreciate the help and encouragement lovingly offered by my wife, Donna. This book is as much hers as mine. She spent countless hours researching subjects and preparing detailed directions to each destination. In addition, she was my constant companion and guide as we crisscrossed the state, visiting each subject described here. Whenever the going got rough, she always found a way to keep me on track. We make a great team.

Introduction

Georgia is blessed with a cornucopia of natural wonders, which are scattered across the length and breadth of the state. Some of these treasures can be found in unlikely places, such as almost within the shadows of the skyscrapers in the state's largest city or along a busy interstate highway. Others can be enjoyed in more natural settings, like the white-sand beaches of the barrier islands off the Georgia coast or an isolated shoal on a beautiful river.

While the sheer number and diversity of these special places, things, and events are overwhelming, remarkably, most weekend adventurers don't know they exist. Even the most avid nature enthusiast rarely has the time to unearth even a fraction of the wealth of wild places and things found in Georgia.

This book is packed with all the information needed to enjoy fifty-two exciting Georgia nature getaways. These weekend adventures have been carefully selected to appeal to travelers with a broad range of interests, including wildlife, fish, wildflowers, fossils, and astronomy.

One of the best ways to heighten the enjoyment of a nature weekend is by becoming familiar with what you hope to see. For example, while seeing hundreds of thousands of blackbirds converging on a roost is breathtaking, one can't help but ask the question, "Why do birds flock together?" It seems that the more we see and experience, the more we want to know.

Since most travelers won't have the luxury of having an expert guide at their sides when they visit these fifty-two nature weekends, each trip description includes a wealth of fascinating natural history information and even some of the legends swirling around each site and/or its wild inhabitants.

How to Use This Book

This book is designed to provide the nature adventurer with everything he or she needs to know to have a memorable outdoor experience. It not only tells you where it go, it also provides directions on how to get there, when to make your visit, operating hours, special regulations, admission fees, amount of time needed to fully enjoy the trip, and what special equipment you will need, if any. (The minimum time commitment does *not* include time needed to get to the site.) The availability of nearby lodging and restaurants is also included.

Even though every effort has been made to provide the reader with the best information available, nature is often unpredictable. Bird or butterfly migrations can occur earlier or later than expected. Flowers sometimes don't bloom on schedule. For this reason it is always a good idea to call ahead and find out what is going on. With this in mind, the names, addresses, and telephone numbers of those agencies that can offer the latest information are listed.

In addition, when you arrive at an area, take the time to stop and talk with the staff managing the site. They are an invaluable source of information. A few minutes spent talking with them can save you hours later on.

Realistic Expectations

An important point to keep in mind when you embark on these nature weekends is that you are a visitor to a natural area; you are not taking a trip to a zoo. When you visit a zoo to see lions, you know when you leave home that you will see a lion. Conversely, when you visit a park or wildlife refuge to see fox squirrels, white-tailed deer, or other animals, realize that you may not see the animals that you traveled so far to observe. Remember, you are dealing with wild animals that come and go at will. By the same token, expect the unexpected. You may, for example, not see the trophy trout you traveled so far to see. Instead, you may cross paths with a black bear.

In other words, don't let the success of your trip hinge solely on whether you spot the animal you are seeking. While you may be disappointed that you didn't find the animal you wanted to see, take pleasure in the things you did encounter.

Be Responsible

With more people than ever before enjoying nature, the chance of our fragile wildlife and plant resources being loved to death has become a major problem. This has caused land managers to enforce regulations designed to reduce the destructive impact of nature enthusiasts.

Whenever visiting wild places, abide by the area's rules and regulations and don't do anything to harm the environment or the plants and animals that live there. Stay on designated trails and viewing platforms. Resist the temptation to pick or dig wild plants. Also, never harass or feed wildlife.

If we all do our part to keep wild places unspoiled and wildlife wild, we can ensure that future generations of nature enthusiasts will be able to enjoy the bounty of the natural world.

A Final Note

As you visit the places described in this volume, you will quickly learn that Georgia is a state of unparalleled natural beauty. My family and I thoroughly enjoyed visiting these special places—I know you will, too.

Map Legend

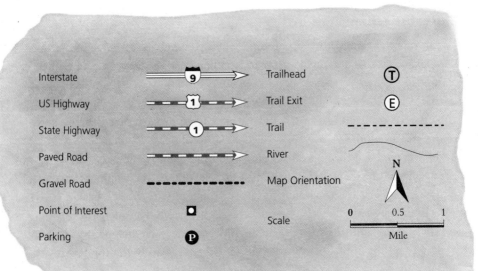

Interstate		Trailhead	T
US Highway		Trail Exit	E
State Highway		Trail	
Paved Road		River	
Gravel Road		Map Orientation	N
Point of Interest		Scale	0 0.5 1
Parking			Mile

Locator Map

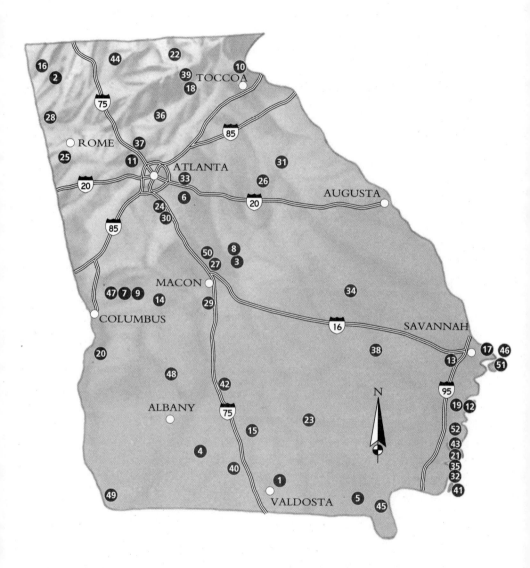

1

A World Apart

One of Georgia's largest Carolina Bays, Grand Bay offers opportunities to observe some of the state's most interesting flora and fauna.

Recommended time: Mid-March through April.

Name and location of site: Grand Bay, a little more than 15 miles from Valdosta.

Minimum time commitment: One to two hours.

What to bring: Binoculars, spotting scope, camera, field guides to both birds and plants.

Admission fee: None.

Directions: From the junction of I–75 (exit 22) and US 41, north of Valdosta, turn left (east) on US 41 and travel 5.9 miles to the junction of US 221. Turn left on US 221 and continue for 8.3 miles to the junction of US 221 and Knights Academy Road. Turn left on Knights Academy Road and travel 1.5 miles to the entrance to the Grand Bay Wildlife Management Area. Turn right at the management area sign and follow the signs to the boardwalk.

The background: Grand Bay is part of the Grand Bay Wildlife Management Area. The area is located on the Moody Air Force Base, an important pilot training facility for the U.S. Air Force. This 9,416-acre management area is truly a multiuse facility. While the area is managed primarily for deer, small game, and waterfowl hunting, the area offers much more.

The Grand Bay Wetland Education Center is a focal point of conservation

What Is a Carolina Bay?

Carolina Bays are distinctively teardrop-shaped wetlands that are found primarily in southeast Georgia and North and South Carolina. These wetlands are shallow (5 to 30 feet deep) depressions filled with peat. They range in size from a few hundred feet to more than 5 miles in length.

Carolina Bays are ancient wetlands that were formed perhaps 250,000 years ago. While nobody is certain how the strange oval depressions were formed, one fanciful theory suggests that they were the result of a giant meteor shower that fell in this area millions of years ago.

Originally a thousand or so Carolina Bays, encompassing a quarter of a million acres of land, dotted the Georgia landscape. During the past century, many of these unique wetlands have been drained and then timber cut. Today Grand Bay remains as one of the largest Carolina Bays in existence.

Some Carolina Bays retain standing water through the year; others, however, periodically dry up. During dry periods, fires have historically burned away rank vegetation and layers of peat and helped maintain areas of open water.

During the nineteenth and early part of the twentieth century, many Carolina Bays were logged. During this time, virgin stands of cypress trees hundreds of years old were cut with two-man saws and hauled to sawmills.

Carolina Bays are home to a variety of wildlife, including redfin and chain pickerel, fliers, largemouth bass, warmouth, cottonmouths, pig frogs, raccoons, and white-tailed deer. In addition, the bays are used by migratory birds, including waterfowl and songbirds, as places to stop and feed or as sites to spend the winter.

education in south Georgia. In addition, a 2,000-foot boardwalk and a 50-foot observation tower allow outdoor recreationists the opportunity to venture into the inner recesses of the bay without ever getting their feet wet. Canoeists also enjoy paddling along a 3-mile canoe trail that winds through the wetland.

Water in the bay is managed through the use of water-control structures that allow managers to regulate water levels within the bay. Water-level management is critical to maintaining the bay's fragile communities.

In recent years sandhill cranes were captured in Florida and brought to this site in order to establish a nesting population of the birds. They were kept in large pens for a brief period of acclimation and then released into the bay. In addition, hundreds of greater sandhill cranes winter in and around the bay. Ring-necked, wood, and other ducks also winter in this wildlife haven.

One of the most interesting denizens of the bay is the round-tailed muskrat or Florida water rat. Until wildlife technicians and biologists discovered these mammals within Grand Bay, experts thought that the animal's range within the Peach State was limited to the area in and around the Okefenokee National Wildlife Refuge far to the east.

The bay also contains a large bird rookery. Here anhingas, great egrets,

A view of the boardwalk from the observation tower

great blue herons, and other waterbirds annually nest in the hundreds. In the winter, the area is also used as a roost by white ibis and other wading birds.

The fun: While Grand Bay is a great place to visit any time of year, there is no better time than late winter and early spring. This is a time of transition. Some of the birds that have wintered here and at points farther south are moving northward. Others remain in their usual winter haunts. Plants that have been dormant all winter are beginning to bloom or sprout new leaves. In addition, temperatures are moderate and humidity is low.

Your adventure begins as soon as you turn off the highway onto the Grand Bay Wildlife Management Area entrance road. As you slowly make your way down this gravel road, be alert for wildlife. White-tailed deer, fox squirrels, and other animals can often be seen along the roadside. Turtles, wood ducks, and wading birds can be spotted in roadside ditches.

Once you have reached the parking lot near the beginning of the board-walk, look at the large pond cypress log displayed beside the education center. This display dramatically demonstrates human impact on the bay. The massive log was cut from a tree felled in the bay around 1910. The log's rings show that, at the time it was cut, the tree was 607 years old. This means that it sprouted about A.D. 1290. Logging forever changed the complexion of the bay. Today the oldest pond cypresses you will see are less than ninety years old.

Before setting foot on the boardwalk, pick up a copy of the free trail guide at the education center. This brochure provides brief descriptions of the eleven numbered stops marked along the boardwalk. It will help you understand what you are viewing as you make your way to the interior of the bay.

As you walk down the trail you will pass through several different types of habitats. The first that you will encounter is a wet savanna. Look for pitcher plants blooming here. You will then pass through a series of different habitats, including a shrub bog, blackgum cypress swamp, and cypress gum pond, before reaching what is perhaps the most picturesque habitat—the prairie. This open marshy area is covered with water from 1 inch to 3 feet deep. This area is best viewed from atop the 50-foot observation tower. From here the panoramic beauty of the bay is truly breathtaking. This vulture-eye view of the bay allows you to enjoy vistas far out into the prairie. One of the most fascinating sights is the rookery directly in front of the tower. Here, great blue herons, anhingas, great egrets, and other waterbirds nest. The rookery is best viewed with a spotting scope. While you will undoubtedly see more birds than any other kind of wildlife, keep an eye peeled for the reptiles and amphibians that live in the bay. Water snakes, frogs, turtles, water moccasins, and even alligators are commonly seen.

While the trail guide directs your attention to most of the major features that can be seen from the trail, many other fascinating things are not included. For example, while wood duck nest boxes are mentioned, prothonotary warbler nesting boxes are not. If you keep your eyes and ears open, you will find a host of plants and animals as well as other features that will leave you leafing through your field guides trying to figure out what you are looking at.

Food and lodging: A good selection of restaurants can be found within 20 miles of the bay.

For more information:
Game Management Section
1773-A Bowen's Mill Highway
Fitzgerald, GA 31750
(229) 426–5267

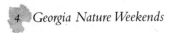

2

A Floral Wonderland

There are few places in Georgia where wildflower enthusiasts will find a more lush assemblage of our diverse and fascinating wildflowers than The Pocket.

Recommended time: Late March through April.

Name and location of site: The Shirley Miller Wildflower Trail at the Crockford–Pigeon Mountain Wildlife Management Area, about 15 miles from Lafayette.

Minimum time commitment: One to two hours.

What to bring: Camera, wildflower guide, hand lens.

Admission fee: None.

Directions: In Lafayette, turn left on US 27 Business and drive 0.3 mile to the junction of US 193. Turn right (west/north) and travel 8.1 miles to Davis Cross Roads. At Davis Cross Roads, turn left onto McLemore Cove Road. Travel 2.5 miles south on McLemore Cove Road to the junction of Hog Jowl Road. Turn left on Hog Jowl Road and go 2.6 miles to Pocket Road. Turn left on Pocket Road and travel 1.2 miles to the parking lot.

The background: The Shirley Miller Wildflower Trail is located in a north-facing cove named The Pocket within the boundaries of the 14,418-acre Crockford–Pigeon Mountain Wildlife Management Area (WMA). The WMA is managed by the Georgia Department of Natural Resources's Wildlife Resources Division. The area is named for a former director of the Wildlife Resources Division, Jack Crockford, and the mountain that makes

Bluebells, shown here, are just one of the more than two dozen species of wildflower that can be viewed along the Shirley Miller Wildflower Trail.

up much of the area. The mountain was named Pigeon Mountain because thousands of passenger pigeons are said to have roosted here during the 1800s.

The Crockford–Pigeon Mountain WMA is the state's best example of a multiuse outdoor recreational area. Each year thousands of Georgians make the trek to the area to enjoy a diversity of outdoor activities such as hunting, hang gliding, caving, biking, horseback riding, birding, wildflower observation, photography, and rock climbing.

The wildflower trail consists of an 800-foot, barrier-free boardwalk spanning part of a cove within The Pocket. The boardwalk allows wildflower enthusiasts to photograph and enjoy the wildflowers without walking on the fragile plants. Prior to the construction of the boardwalk, this precious stand of wildflowers was being trampled by visitors.

The fun: Wildflowers are among the most beautiful of our natural treasures and come in a kaleidoscope of colors. Here, at the base of a steep hardwood ridge, some two dozen species of wildflowers can be easily seen from the boardwalk. Some of the wildflowers that can be found here include Virginia bluebells, yellow poppy, trout lily, trillium (three species), common toadshade, spring beauty, toothwort (two species), hepatica, bloodroot, blue cohosh, columbine, Canada waterleaf, and wild hyacinth.

Observing wildflowers is totally different from wildlife watching. Often we have only a fleeting glimpse of a deer or bird before it disappears into the forest. Since wildflowers don't move, we can take our time studying and photographing them. The closer you examine a wildflower, the more you will be impressed with the delicate beauty that is inherent to each plant.

As you walk along the trail, a series of interpretive signs will enhance your experience. The large sign at the beginning of the trail is particularly helpful as it illustrates, in color, many of the striking wildflowers that you will see along the boardwalk. However, since some plants growing along the trail are not depicted on the sign, it is a good idea to bring your own field guide.

Since all these wildflowers don't bloom at the same time, plan on taking several trips to the area. This will allow you to see the blooming of the greatest variety of wildflowers.

As you slowly walk the trail, listen and look for birds. Since the spring migration occurs during the spring wildflower blooming season, you may find a host of migratory songbirds. Louisiana waterthrushes can usually be heard calling along the small stream that meanders along the edge of the wildflower area. Permanent residents such as woodpeckers, titmice, and chickadees can also be heard and seen. It is always a treat to hear the sound of a turkey gobbling reverberate through The Pocket.

Food and lodging: Fifteen restaurants and four hotels are found within 15 miles of the site.

For more information:

Game Management Section
Route 1, Floyd Springs Road
Armuchee, GA 30105
(706) 295–6041

3

Spring

A Blue and White Tapestry

The two plants—flowering dogwood and Chinese wisteria—that create the floral tapestry at the Piedmont National Wildlife Refuge are as different as they are beautiful.

Recommended time: Mid-March through mid-April.

Name and location of site: Piedmont National Wildlife Refuge, about 15 miles from Forsyth.

Minimum time commitment: One to two hours.

What to bring: Camera, binoculars, field guide to wildflowers.

Admission fee: None.

Directions: From Forsyth: From the junction of I–75 (exit 186) and Juliette Road, head east 13.4 miles on Juliette Road to the junction of Round Oak–Juliette Road and Jarrell Plantation Road. Turn left on Round Oak–Juliette Road. The floral display is staged on both sides of the road from this intersection to the entrance road to the Piedmont National Wildlife Refuge Visitor Center.

The background: Spring provides us with a succession of one spectacular floral show after another. In late March and early April, ravishing displays of azaleas, dogwoods, and cherries in backyards and parks throughout middle Georgia vie for our attention along with the eye-catching productions being staged in woodlands throughout the region.

One of the best examples of these floral quilts, created by violet-blue swatches of wisterias and the white of dogwoods, is found along the county road that meanders through the Piedmont National Wildlife Refuge. Here an

Chinese Wisteria on the Loose

The Chinese wisteria was introduced into this country decades ago as an ornamental. As such, it was commonly planted in the yards surrounding homesites. Although all that remains of many of these farmsteads are sentinel-like chimneys, the wisterias that once adorned these homes have escaped cultivation. Today Chinese and other Asian varieties of wisteria have become serious pest plants in many parts of Georgia. Being prolific and able to grow in a wide range of soil types, their escape into our woodlands was easy. Since Chinese wisteria does best in full sun, its floral splendor often reaches its pinnacle along our roadsides.

The Chinese wisteria often chokes out native plants. In addition, being a leguminous plant (a plant that puts nitrogen in the soil), it increases soil fertility. This is sometimes harmful to native species that have adapted to poor soil types.

Although this woody vine is potentially a problem, when kept under control it can be a beautiful addition to your yard. Depending on how you prune the plant, it can be grown as a vine or trained into a shrub or tree.

abundance of dogwood trees, in full bloom, can be seen far out in the open pine woodlands that hug the road. The stark white of the dogwoods' blooms is accentuated by the rich green of pine boughs and dark hues of the trunks of pine trees. Along the highway, blankets of grapelike clusters of wisteria blooms cascade from the tops of the trees.

The fun: The best way to enjoy the dazzling color of the wisterias and dogwoods is to slowly drive down Round Oak–Juliette Road. Whenever you find an area that appeals to you, pull off the road. For the most part road shoulders are wide and firm. By stopping your car and getting out to enjoy the view, you also have the opportunity to enjoy the sweet scent of the wisteria blooms and the calls and songs of the songbirds that abound in the forest along the road. Some birds that you should see and hear are the pine warbler, yellow-throated vireo, red-eyed vireo, tufted titmouse, Kentucky warbler, prairie warbler, Carolina chickadee, Northern parula, and others.

If you look carefully, you will also find other trees, shrubs, and wildflowers blooming near the road. If you make your trip in March, chances are good that redbud will also be blooming. The redbud is a small tree that doesn't have red buds or blooms. However, each spring its branches are festooned with clusters of pealike flowers that can best be described as dark pink or rose.

Be on the lookout for nectar feeders feeding on the dogwoods and wisterias. While neither plant is known to produce large quantities of nectar, honeybees, bumblebees, butterflies, and hummingbirds will visit them.

When you reach the entrance road to the visitors center, you might want to take a few minutes to visit this facility. The visitors center is open from 9:00 A.M. to 5:00 P.M. Saturday and Sunday. This facility houses excellent dioramas that depict many plants and animals found on the refuge.

After your visit to the visitors center, retrace your route back to the junction of Juliette and Round Oak–Juliette Roads. You will find that, as you travel west, looking at the same woodlands from a different perspective will reveal picturesque views that were not evident as you traveled east.

Since the peak blooming periods for wisteria and dogwood vary from year to year, it is a good idea to call the Piedmont National Wildlife Refuge beforehand.

Food and lodging: More than two dozen restaurants, eleven motels, and a campground can be found within 20 miles of the site.

For more information:
Refuge Manager
Piedmont National Wildlife Refuge
Round Oak, GA 31038
(478) 986–5441

4

A Diet of Fire and Water

Visitors can enjoy the rare beauty of three species of pitcher plants
in one of Georgia's largest remaining pitcher-plant bogs.

Recommended time: April through mid-May.

Name and location of site: The Doerun Pitcher Plant Bog Natural
Area, approximately 3 miles from Doerun and 10 miles from Moultrie.

Minimum time commitment: Two hours.

What to bring: Camera, binoculars, field guide to plants.

Admission fee: None.

Directions: The natural area is located on the left-hand side of SR 133,
approximately 3 miles southeast of Doerun.

The background: Pitcher-plant bogs are among the most fascinating and
threatened habitats found in Georgia. It is estimated that about 97 percent of
the pitcher-plant bogs that were in existence in the late 1800s have disappeared. The Doerun Pitcher Plant Bog remains one of Georgia's largest vestiges of this unusual and harsh habitat.

At Doerun the bogs are found in shallow depressions formed between the
gently sloping hillsides. Rainwater that falls on the surrounding slopes slowly
collects in the bogs. Although small pools of water may persist in the bogs for
several weeks, such areas are few and far between. However, the soils found in
the bog typically remain wet throughout most of the year.

The soils in pitcher-plant bogs are sandy and very acidic (with a pH ranging from 3.5 to 5). They are also low in minerals such as calcium, magnesium,

and potassium. Most plants cannot survive in this nutrient-poor environment. Among the hardy plants that do exist here is a group of plants that is carnivorous. They supplement their need for nutrients by capturing and digesting insects, spiders, and other small animals. Nine species of carnivorous plants live here, including three pitcher plants, one bladderwort, two butterworts, and three sundews.

By far, the showiest of these unique plants are the pitcher plants. At Doerun, you can find parrot, hooded, and yellow flytrap pitcher-plants, which are native to the area. As is the case with all pitcher plants, each has leaves that are modified to form a pitcher topped with a hood. Water and digestive juices collect in the bottom of the pitcher. Insects are lured to the pitcher by nectar produced near the top of the pitcher. Once the insects are inside, the hood helps funnel them downward as they search for nectar. A combination of downward-pointing hairs and the pitcher's smooth interior prevents the insects from crawling out. Eventually the insects tumble into the water and digestive juices pooled at the base of the pitcher. Slowly the insects are digested and their nutrients absorbed by the plant.

The fun: As soon as you turn off the highway, begin looking for the pitcher-plant bog on your left. The bog is tucked into the folds of the gently sloping hillside. Even if you have never visited the bog before, you will be able to recognize it at a glance. It will be blanketed in the bright yellow color of thousands of pitcher plants standing like sentinels in the bog's moist soil. Surrounding the tendrils of the bog is a breathtaking open parklike stand of longleaf pines. The forest floor is carpeted in wiregrass.

The best place to view the bog is from the observation deck found just below the parking area. Here visitors can closely view the plants without getting their feet wet.

See if you can find examples of all three species of pitcher plants in this area. Each plant will have several pitchers and a single blossom that hangs downward like a bell. The flowers of the yellow flytrap and hooded pitcher plants are yellow. The parrot pitcher plant displays a red flower.

The yellow flytrap, or yellow trumpet as it is also called, is the showiest of the three pitcher plants found here. It stands upwards of 3 feet tall.

The hooded pitcher plant looks much like the yellow flytrap; however, it stands only 6 to 12 inches tall. If you look closely, you will be able to see translucent spots near the top of the pitcher. Insects that enter the mouth of the pitcher are often drawn to the light passing through these spots.

The parrot pitcher plant measures roughly 7 inches in diameter. Its 8-inch pitchers are more open than either the yellow flytrap or hooded pitcher plants. In addition, its pitchers are arranged more horizontally than upright. It is thought that this better enables the plant to capture insects when it is flooded.

Look for animals near the pitcher plants. If the plants are in bloom, bumblebees will be making frequent visits to the showy flowers. Bumblebees are the pitcher plants' main pollinators. Both crawling and flying insects can also be seen. If you watch closely, you may see insects unsuspectingly enter the plants' deadly mouths.

As you gaze across the bog and adjacent longleaf pine/wiregrass landscape, you will see evidence that fire has burned across the land in the recent past. Blackened stumps and tree trunks are everywhere. In the bog, the dead stems and branches of shrubs give mute testimony to the fire's destructive power.

Actually, the slow, prescribed fires set by the Wildlife Resources Division are more beneficial than destructive. The fires periodically inching across the landscape benefit the bog and longleaf/pine wiregrass communities. Without fire, shrubs and other hardwoods would encroach into the bog. If allowed to prosper, they would quickly overshadow and eventually displace the sun-loving pitcher plants.

If you would like to explore more of the area, walk the trail leading away from the viewing platform. This trail meanders along the edge of the bog and up the far hillside before leading back to the parking lot. Along the way you may be treated to the sights and sounds of Bachman's sparrows, great-crested flycatchers, pine warblers, woodpeckers, and other birds that inhabit this landscape. The gobbling of turkey gobblers and the *bobwhite* call of the Northern bobwhite can be heard on spring mornings.

The trail also passes by gopher tortoise burrows. If you are lucky, you may encounter a gopher tortoise dining on one of its favorite foods, wiregrass.

Scores of wildflowers grow in the area, including nine species of orchids and four state-protected plants. Since many of these plants grow along the trail, keep your plant-identification guide handy.

Don't pick or dig any pitcher plants or other wildflowers growing in the Doerun Pitcher Plant Bog Natural Area. Also, don't wander off the trail. The trail and observation platform have been developed so that we all can enjoy the pitcher plants and other plants and animals living here without damaging the area's inhabitants and their habitats.

Food and lodging: Travelers can find three motels and five restaurants in Moultrie, approximately 10 miles from the area.

For more information:
Nongame Wildlife/Natural Heritage Section
Wildlife Resources Division
2117 US Highway 278 SE
Social Circle, GA 30279
(770) 918–6411 (when calling from Atlanta) or (770) 557–3032 (when calling from outside Atlanta)

5

The Roar of the Alligator

This unusual adventure with alligators is more geared toward listening for wildlife than viewing it.

Recommended time: April through May (peak mid-April).

Name and location of site: Stephen C. Foster State Park, less than 20 miles from Fargo.

Minimum time commitment: Six hours, but it's best to plan to spend the night in the park.

What to bring: Tape recorder, flashlight, camera, binoculars, insect repellent.

Admission fee: Since this park is in a National Wildlife Refuge, visitors are required to pay a $5.00-per-car entrance fee instead of using a Georgia ParkPass. The fee is good for seven days. Free admission is granted to holders of a current federal Golden Eagle Passport or federal Migratory Bird Hunting and Conservation Stamp (duck stamp).

Directions: In Fargo, turn left on SR 177 and continue 18 miles to the park.

The background: The American alligator is the ruler of the Okefenokee Swamp. This formidable monarch is the largest reptile in North America and capable of reaching 19 feet in length and more than 850 pounds in weight. However, adult males typically average slightly more than 11 feet in length, and adult females are about 9 feet.

Throughout most of the year alligators reign over this domain in silence. However, during April and May the bellows of adult alligators are reminders that they are patrolling their realm.

Spring is the alligators' breeding season, and the males roar to warn other alligators to stay away from their breeding territories as well as to attract mates. It is part of an involved courtship that includes other sounds, bubble blowing, nose-taps, and rubbing.

Both male and female alligators roar. Extremely large adult males make the deepest, loudest bellows. When nights are still, these resonating roars can be heard a mile away. These vocalizations are produced by air rushing across the alligator's vocal cords. When an alligator gets ready to bellow, with its mouth closed it will thrust its head and tail out of the water and inflate its throat like a balloon. Just before the roar is heard, the animal's body rapidly vibrates. This causes water surrounding its scaly form to dance upward making the animal appear like it is the centerpiece of an elaborate water fountain.

The fun: Due to the unusual nature of this adventure, plan on arriving at the park by noon and staying in the park through the night. This will give you an opportunity to scout the area and find the best places to listen for the alligators. Alligators begin roaring about the time the park is closing down for the day and continue through early morning. The last thing you want is to be caught inside the park's gate without having made provisions for spending the night. Before you embark on your adventure, find out when the gate closes. The staff at the park is extremely helpful and can offer tips that will help ensure the success of your quest.

Two areas that you will want to investigate in search of the alligators are the nature trail and the access road found along the east side of the canal leading from the boat basin to Billy's Lake. Look for alligators suspended in the water or basking on the shoreline. Keep in mind that only adult alligators bellow. Identify an adult alligator by its size—they are usually at least 6 feet long.

The entrance to the nature trail is on the west side of the boat basin. The focal point of the trail is a 2,100-foot boardwalk that allows visitors to explore this watery world without getting their feet wet.

For a real treat take a boat trip into the swamp. You can bring your own or rent a boat or canoe at the Trading Post. A boat will allow you to explore miles of waterways that meander through the swamp. Typically, on a boat trip into the swamp you will see alligators, turtles, snakes, songbirds, wading birds, and other wildlife.

When you venture into the swamp by boat, keep in mind that you have to be back at the dock before dark. It is easy to lose track of time and end up too far from the boat dock to make it back by sundown.

When darkness begins to descend on this area, nicknamed Land of Trembling Earth, you need to be stationed at the place you feel will offer your greatest chance of hearing alligator roars. It will not be difficult to pick out this unique sound from a cacophony of calls made by owls, insects, frogs, and toads. This strange sound is described as a throaty, drawn-out roar. To some the roar sounds much like a prolonged snore.

Food and lodging: Travelers will find sixty-six tent, trailer, and RV sites and nine cottages at Stephen C. Foster State Park. Two motels and a restaurant are located in Fargo.

For more information:
Stephen Foster State Park
Route 1, Box 131
Fargo, GA 31631
(912) 637–5274

6

The Lilliputian Plant World
of Panola Mountain

Some of Georgia's hardiest and smallest plants grow on these granite mountain outcrops.

Recommended time: Late March through April.

Name and location of site: Panola Mountain State Conservation Park, 10.5 miles (fifteen minutes) southeast of Atlanta.

Minimum time commitment: One to two hours.

What to bring: Camera, binoculars.

Admission fee: Daily parking fee $2.00 per vehicle; an annual Georgia ParkPass is $25. Discounts are available for senior citizens.

Directions: From Atlanta: From the junction of I–285 and I–20, travel east 2.9 miles on I–20 to Wesley Chapel Road (exit 68). Turn right (south) onto Wesley Chapel Road and drive 0.4 mile to the junction of Snapfinger Road. Turn left onto Snapfinger Road and continue south 7.2 miles to the entrance to Panola Mountain State Conservation Park, on your left.

The background: Standing beside a granite outcrop and gazing down at the tiny plants growing there, it is easy to imagine that you are visiting the mythical island of Lilliput made famous in Jonathan Swift's fanciful book *Gulliver's Travels.* Like the small inhabitants of Swift's strange island, these lilliputian plants are often overlooked.

Rock outcrops are among Georgia's harshest habitats. They are subject to extreme fluctuations in both temperature and moisture. The thin soils that are

The delicate beauty of the tiny diamorpha plants can only be appreciated when viewed close-up.

found in shallow depressions on these rocky sites are poor in nutrients. Remarkably, these severe habitats are home to a hardy group of plants and animals that is well adapted to live here.

Georgia's rock outcrops are ideal places to see and learn about the earliest stages of plant succession. One of the showiest of these plants is a tiny succulent plant called diamorpha. In spring this small red plant blankets portions of the rock outcrops on which it grows. Later in the year, when temperatures rise and water becomes increasingly scarce, diamorpha begins losing its reddish hue.

The 633-acre Panola Mountain State Conservation Park is widely recognized by conservationists as having Georgia's best managed granite outcrops. These outcrops are found on Panola Mountain, a one hundred-acre granite mountain (monadnock). Here the Georgia Parks, Recreation and Historic Sites Division is protecting the fragile granite outcrop communities while at the same time using them for recreation and education.

The park has a picnic area, an interpretive center, and hiking trails. Three of the trails (Rock Outcrop Trail, Fitness Trail, and Microwatershed Trail) are

Plant Succession

The process by which one plant community replaces another in an orderly fashion is called plant succession. Although plant succession is going on all around us, it isn't often that we get a chance to see primary succession in action such as it is on Panola Mountain's rock outcrops.

Primary succession begins on bare surfaces like rock outcrops. Secondary succession takes place in areas that have been altered. For example, the succession that takes place after a forest has been clearcut would be secondary succession.

Each stage in succession is called a sere. Seres are often named for the plants that dominate during each step in the successional process. Examples of some of the several stages for the Georgia Piedmont where Panola Mountain is located would be the herbaceous, shrub, and woody plant.

The reason why one community is succeeded by another is simple. As each community dominates a piece of land for a time, the environment in which they live gradually changes. As these changes take place, the environment becomes less optimum for the plants that are currently growing there. Since the new conditions favor the growth of other plants, over time the new plants take over the site. However, as the years go by, they too will be replaced by another plant community.

The final community in succession is called the climax. Unless altered by humans or another force, this community remains relatively unchanged over long periods of time. The climax community at Panola Mountain is the Oak/ Hickory Forest.

As might be expected, certain animals associate themselves with different stages of succession. For example, on Panola Mountain, certain mites, collops beetles, and ants dominate the Diamorpha Community. However, in the nearby climax forest, red-eyed vireos and other forest-dwelling birds are found.

open to the public. The Fitness Trail is 1 mile long and was designed with physical-fitness enthusiasts in mind. Another 3.5-mile trail is only used for guided tours. Guided hikes are scheduled throughout the year. However, if you are interested in seeing the plants at their most showy, you need to go in March.

The fun: The best place to begin your adventure is at the interpretive center. Here you will find a display that depicts and describes the plant and animal communities found on Panola Mountain's granite outcrops. The themes of the other displays are rocks of the area, backyard wildlife, and forest animals. The interpretive center also houses a butterfly collection, an active beehive, and a live bat exhibit.

The rock outcrop communities can be best appreciated by taking the guided 3.5-mile tour offered every weekend. Call the park office for times. The tours take you into a section of the park that can only be visited with interpretive guides.

If you don't want to take the guided tour, your next best choice would be the Rock Outcrop Trail; its trailhead is directly behind the interpretive center. This is a moderately steep trail that is 0.75 mile long.

As you walk around the building toward the trailhead, take a few moments to look at the backyard habitat demonstration area at the rear of the building. This well-done interpretive feature displays various nesting boxes, feeders, birdhouses, and plants that can be used to attract wildlife to a backyard.

Continue on the path to the junction of the Microwatershed and Rock Outcrop Trails. Take the left fork and begin your walk down the Rock Outcrop Trail. The trail will wind through an oak/hickory forest. Interpretive signage along the way identifies various plants and other natural features. Small teaching stations along the trail are reached by short trails branching off the main trail.

Look for red buckeyes and crossvine blooming along the trail. The colorful flowers of these two plants are sources of nectar for hummingbirds, butterflies, and other nectar feeders in spring.

Soon after the trail makes a swing to the west, you will see a rock outcrop on your right. The trail courses around the edge of the outcrop. A boardwalk, overlook, and fencing protect the fragile outcrop vegetation from trampling.

When you first look at the outcrop, you'll notice the small patches of reddish plants called diamorpha. Most of these plants grow well away from the boardwalk; however, if you look carefully, you will find some growing close to the trail. If you closely examine these inches-tall plants, you will find that they bear tiny white blooms.

Lichens (small, scaly grayish-green plants) grow in small patches on the exposed rock surfaces. These primitive plants slowly transform the rock into soil. In the shallow depressions found in the rocks, three distinct communities exist. The depths of the shallow soils found in these depressions largely determines which communities can survive there. The simplest community is called the Diamorpha Community and basically consists of only two plants—the small reddish diamorpha and lichens. These plants are able to live in some of the most inhospitable portions of the outcrop and exist in shallow rocky depressions where the soil is less than 3.5 inches deep. Due to high temperatures and little moisture, few, if any, living plants can live here during the summer and fall.

The Lichen and Moss Community is found in areas where soils are a little deeper (up to slightly more than 5 inches deep). Here lichens and diamorpha plants grow alongside hardy moss, Confederate daisies, and pineweed. If you want to see these plants in bloom, you must return in the summer.

In those locations where soils reach a depth of a little less than 15 inches, you will find the greatest plant diversity. This community is called the Annual-Perennial Herb Community. Here you will find the same plant types found in both the Lichen and Moss and the Diamorpha Communities as well as grasses like broomsedge, groundsel, and sunnybells.

For millions of years plants have been colonizing bare rock and slowly helping create soil here. As you look at this unhospitable environment keep in mind that this agonizingly slow process of soil formation has been going on here for an estimated fifteen million years. If you have any question that the process is successful, simply look at the forest that blankets much of Panola Mountain. Without soil formation and plant succession, the forest would not exist.

Food and lodging: Numerous restaurants and motels are found within 30 miles of the site.

For more information:
Panola Mountain State Conservation Park
2600 Highway 155 SW
Stockbridge, GA 30281
(470) 389–7801

7

A Medley of Spring Wildflowers

*Wildflower enthusiasts will find many of their favorites in the
diverse native plant collection in these gardens.*

Recommended time: March through April.

Name and location of site: The Meadowlark Gardens Area
Wildflower Trail at Callaway Gardens, just outside Pine Mountain.

Minimum time commitment: One hour.

What to bring: Camera, binoculars, field guide to wildflowers.

Admission fee: One-day adult admission, $12; one-day child (ages six to
twelve) admission $6.00.

Directions: In Pine Mountain, at the junction of SR 354 and US 27, turn
right onto SR 354 and continue west approximately 0.5 mile to the entrance
of Callaway Gardens, on your left.

The background: Each spring thousands of people make pilgrimages to
Georgia's woodlands in hopes of finding their favorite wildflowers in bloom.
Since the ranges of these colorful plants are often limited to certain parts of
the state, wildflower enthusiasts often have to travel hundreds of miles to
enjoy the beauty of their favorites.

At the Meadowlark Gardens Area Wildflower Trail, horticulturalists have
skillfully arranged a collection of more than seventy species of native flowering
trees, shrubs, and wildflowers from Georgia and throughout the Southeast.
During a brief walk along this 0.75-mile trail, you can see wildflowers that
would normally require you to travel throughout the region to enjoy.

Trilliums can be seen growing along the trail.

The trail is located at Callaway Gardens, which is operated by the nonprofit Ida Cason Callaway Foundation.

The fun: The spring wildflowers growing along the Meadowlark Gardens Area Wildflower Trail have two flowering peaks. The first peak occurs in early March, long before the forests have donned their mantles of green. During these often chilly, windy days, the first harbingers of spring announce that the seasons are changing. Some of the colorful flowers that festoon the forest floor at this time of year are bluebells, spring beauty, toothwort, trout lily, birdfoot violet, celandine poppy, rue anemone, hepatica, and bloodroot. As you walk among the leafless trees guarding the trail at this time of year, it is not uncommon to find twenty-five species of wildflowers blooming.

If you return to the trail in mid-April, you will find that Mother Nature has closed the curtain on the first act of her spring production. Now the set is decorated with various shades of green created by the tender green leaves that adorn every tree and shrub. The forest floor is mottled with patches of shade and sunlight. The stars of this act are the native azaleas, columbine, fire pink, mountain laurel, red buckeye, mayapple, and a host of others.

The wide, gently winding trail that begins beside the Pioneer Cabin leads you through a variety of habitats typical of this Piedmont region of Georgia. As you might expect, each habitat, whether it is a ravine, hillside, or meadow, has its own characteristic wildflowers. In addition, you have the unique opportunity to see wildflowers (often identified with small markers) growing as they would in both the mountain and coastal plain regions of the state.

One of the most dramatic changes that takes place between early March and mid-April at the gardens is the birds that you will encounter. The birds seen during your initial trip will be a combination of permanent residents such as tufted titmouse, Carolina chickadee, and downy woodpecker and wintering birds including ruby-crowned kinglet and yellow-bellied sapsucker. In mid-April most of the wintering birds will have moved northward. In their place you will find that the year-round residents are sharing the woodlands with spring migrants such as great-crested flycatchers and wood thrushes.

Also look for fish living in the trailside pond. Frogs and toads inhabit the area. While mammals live here, besides an occasional squirrel, most mammals will be difficult to find. However, look for the tracks of opossums, raccoons, deer, and other mammals in the moist soil along the trail.

Regardless of how many times you walk the trail, you will continually make new discoveries.

Food and lodging: More than two dozen restaurants, eleven hotels, four bed-and-breakfasts, and two campgrounds are found within 5 miles of the trail.

For more information:

Education Department
Callaway Gardens
P.O. Box 2000
Pine Mountain, GA 31822
(800) CALLAWAY (to reach the Education Department, take option 4, then option 2)

8

The Spring Serenade of the Wild Turkey

*Hone your wildlife-listening skills as you travel this wildlife drive
in search of the turkey's gobble and other bird calls.*

Recommended time: Late March through May. The drive is open during daylight hours only.

Name and location of site: The Little Rock Wildlife Drive, approximately 15 miles from Forsyth.

Minimum time commitment: Two to three hours.

What to bring: Binoculars; field guides to birds, tracks, and wildflowers; camera; insect repellent.

Admission fee: None.

Directions: From Forsyth, at the junction of I–75 (exit 186) and Juliette Road, head east 13.4 miles to the junction of Round Oak–Juliette Road and Jarrell Plantation Road. Turn left on Round Oak–Juliette Road and drive 2.4 miles to the entrance of The Little Rock Wildlife Drive. Turn right onto the drive and begin your adventure.

The background: One of the most fascinating sounds in the wild is the gobble of a turkey gobbler. It is a sound that even captivated the imagination of Native Americans whose war whoop is said to be an imitation of a gobble.

Male turkeys, called gobblers, gobble to let hen turkeys know that they are looking for mates. It also tells other gobblers that potential rivals for the hens' attention are also in the area. While gobbling can be heard throughout the year, by far, gobbling most often reverberates through the Georgia woodlands in the spring.

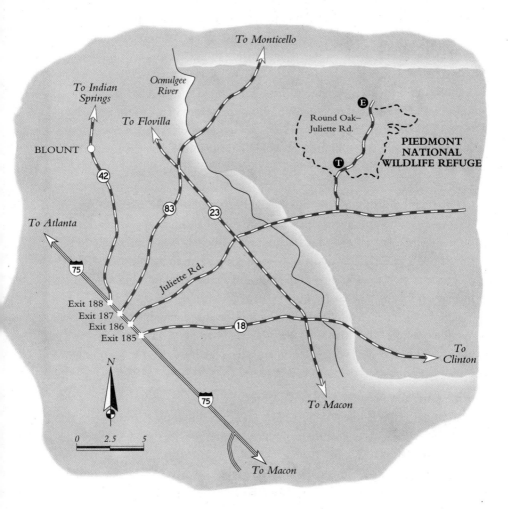

To Monticello

To Indian Springs

Ocmulgee River

To Flovilla

BLOUNT

(42)

Round Oak–Juliette Rd.

E

PIEDMONT NATIONAL WILDLIFE REFUGE

T

To Atlanta

(83) (23)

(75)

Juliette Rd.

Exit 188
Exit 187
Exit 186
Exit 185

(18)

To Clinton

N

0   2.5   5

(75)

To Macon

To Macon

During the spring breeding season there are two peaks in gobbling activity. One peak occurs in late March, when a few hens are ready to leave their winter flocks to mate. Gobbling peaks at this time because gobblers have to vie with one another for the few hens willing to abandon their flocks. As the hens become more willing to mate, the gobblers have an easier time finding available hens. The second gobbling peak takes place in late April. By that time, the dogwood trees have dropped their petals and most of the hens are nesting. Again, faced with a shortage of mates, the gobblers kick up their gobbling a few notches.

This is perhaps the best time to hear gobbling as the gobblers will often sound off at any loud noise. Anything from the sound of a passing jet, a dog barking, or the slamming of a car door can set them off. Weather also affects gobbling. Usually you will hear less gobbling on cloudy days than when the skies are clear. While turkeys gobble less while it is raining, it picks up between showers.

On a typical spring morning, gobbling begins while the turkeys are still on the roost. By the time the sun has been up for a half hour, gobbling is already on the decline. It will continue to diminish as the day wears on, reaching its lowest point in early afternoon, only to pick up again in early evening.

The very best time to hear gobbling is on a clear, still morning when it has not rained for the past twelve hours.

The Little Rock Wildlife Drive is located on the Piedmont National Wildlife Refuge. The drive follows a graveled road for 4.8 miles. Two-way traffic is allowed only as far as the pond, after which the road is open only to one-way traffic.

The fun: Your adventure begins as soon as you pass through the gate at the head of the Little Rock Wildlife Drive. Look for the display on the right side of the road. Pick up one of the pamphlets, which provides the history of the Piedmont National Wildlife Refuge as well as information about each of the twelve stops marked with turkey symbols along the drive. At the end of the trail you will find a wood-duck nesting box on the left side of the road. If you don't wish to keep your pamphlet, deposit it in the box so that others can use it.

The best way to hear turkeys gobbling is to stop at least every 0.2 mile along the trail. At each stop get out of your car and listen for three to five minutes. If you don't hear a turkey, move on. Drive very slowly between stops with your windows down. You never know when you might hear a gobbler.

A turkey gobbler in full strut

One of the best places to hear and see turkeys is in the area called Little Rock, stop four on the tour. Scan the fields for turkeys. You might see a gobbler with his tail fanned as he struts before his flock of hens. If you happen to spot turkeys, stay in your car. Your car makes an ideal blind.

Little Rock is also a great place to see other wildlife. Canada geese, wood ducks, ring-necked ducks, belted kingfishers, and even deer, otters, and beavers are sometimes seen here.

As you drive from spot to spot, you will hear a host of different kinds of birds calling. On a typical visit you might hear birds such as prairie warblers, tufted titmice, Carolina wrens, Kentucky warblers, Eastern kingbirds, pine warblers, red-bellied woodpeckers, and others. A great way to learn the calls is to try to find the bird calling. Using a pair of binoculars, scan the tree where the call seems to be coming from. With a little practice, you will soon be able to quickly find calling birds. If the bird is not near the road, don't be afraid to venture into the woods to find it. The U.S. Fish and Wildlife Service, the federal agency that manages the refuge, permits to you walk into the woods along the trail. A word of caution: Before going into the woods, spray yourself with insect repellent. Ticks are often quite abundant in spring.

As you make your way along the drive, look for wildflowers. In March redbud, flowering dogwood, and wisteria can be seen. Also, look for mayapple. You can find small stands of this interesting plant on the right-hand side of the road just beyond stop number six and immediately before stop number eleven. Mayapples grow in small groups and have a single white flower that blooms beneath a flat, shieldlike umbrella of deeply lobed leaves.

One of the most interesting stops along the drive is in the area devastated by a tornado on November 22, 1992. This destructive storm cut a swath up to 0.5 mile wide and 8 miles long across the refuge. Some 2,000 acres of timber were destroyed in a matter of minutes when the storm passed through.

After you have finished your tour, turn right at the highway and travel east 1.7 miles to the entrance sign to the Piedmont National Wildlife Refuge Headquarters and Visitor Center. Turn left and drive 0.8 mile to the center. The visitors center is open from 9:00 A.M. to 5:00 P.M. on weekends. Here you will find a three-dimensional model of the forest surrounding the Little Rock Wildlife Drive and other displays showcasing many animals and plants that inhabit the area. One of the best displays shows views of a beaver pond from above and below the water.

Food and lodging: Eleven motels and more than two dozen restaurants can be found within 20 miles of the drive.

For more information:
Refuge Manager
Piedmont National Wildlife Refuge
Round Oak, GA 31038
(478) 985–5441

9

An Explosion of Azaleas

Visitors can enjoy flowering azaleas in two outstanding azalea gardens as well as along a 5-mile scenic drive.

Recommended time: Mid-March through mid-April. Flowering here usually peaks around Easter.

Name and location of site: Overlook Azalea Garden and the Callaway Brothers Azalea Bowl, just outside of Pine Mountain.

Minimum time commitment: Two to three hours.

What to bring: Camera, binoculars, bicycle (optional).

Admission fee: One-day adult admission, $12; One-day child (ages six to twelve) admission, $6.00.

Directions: In Pine Mountain, turn right onto SR 354 and continue west approximately 0.5 mile to the entrance to Callaway Gardens, on the left.

The background: Callaway Gardens is famous for its azaleas. The oldest of the gardens is the Overlook Azalea Garden, which was built in the 1950s. This garden contains 700 different varieties of azaleas. A paved road, bicycle path, and 1.6-mile walking trail traverse this area.

In 1999 the Callaway Brothers Azalea Bowl was unveiled. This forty-acre garden is the largest azalea garden in North America. More than 3,400 hybrid azaleas are planted here. Accenting these plantings are 120 different kinds of trees and shrubs.

The Callaway Brothers Azalea Bowl features a man-made lake and waterfall. A blanket of 1,200 azaleas surrounds the one-acre impoundment, called Mirror Lake.

The Azalea Bowl's 1.2 miles of paved walking paths weave through this sea of color. Benches and a gazebo offer visitors the opportunity to rest and enjoy the grandeur of this picturesque setting.

Native plants are highlighted along the scenic drive. Both native and Asian varieties are used to create the breathtaking floral displays that adorn the two azalea gardens. In fact, hundreds of the azaleas planted in the Azalea Bowl came from cuttings taken from plants growing in the Overlook Azalea Garden.

The fun: It is often said that blooming azaleas epitomize springtime in the south. If this is indeed true, finding a place that is more imbued with the sights of spring would be difficult. At this time of year, azaleas are seemingly everywhere.

There are three ways to enjoy the masses of multihued azaleas. Most people begin by leisurely driving along the scenic drive, slowing down to look at the particularly stunning displays of color. During the peak of the blooming season, traffic can become quite congested. However, few complain about being slowed by traffic when the roadside is ablaze with thousands of azalea blooms. In fact, folks commonly make a second drive through to further savor the bounty of flowers.

If you find that your trip down the scenic drive was only an appetizer, you are now ready for the main course. Next, walk the trails through both the Overlook Azalea Garden and the Callaway Brothers Azalea Bowl. In fact, the only way that you can truly appreciate these gardens is by slowly walking along the trails that wind their way through the gardens. Bring your camera as you will find great photo opportunities around every bend.

Since the plants growing along the trail are identified with discreet signs, you can jot down the names of those varieties that you find particularly pleasing to the eye. If you are considering adding them to your home landscape, note how different colored varieties are blended together in mass plantings.

A walk along the trails will reveal the often subtle beauty of myriad bulbs and other flowering plants interlaced among the azaleas. Many of these plants are native to the Southeast. From a distance their beauty can easily be lost amid the explosions of azalea blooms.

Some of the most stunning sights can be found where the colorful azaleas are reflected on the surfaces of the garden's lakes—Whip-Poor-Will Lake and especially Mirror Lake in the Azalea Bowl.

For many visitors a trip to Callaway Gardens would not be complete with-

In spring, azaleas accent the woodlands.

out bicycling down a portion or all of the more than 7.5 miles of paved bike trails that crisscross the area. You can bring your own bicycle or rent one when you get there.

If you prefer native azaleas to the Asian varieties, you will find twelve different kinds of native azaleas growing at the two azalea gardens and along the scenic drive. As a rule, these plants reach the pinnacle of their blooming cycle after most of the flowers of the Asian forms have withered.

Whether you like to enjoy the beauty of blooming azaleas from your car, from a bicycle, or on foot, this is the place for you.

Food and lodging: More than two dozen restaurants, eleven hotels, four bed-and-breakfasts, and two campgrounds are located within 5 miles of the gardens.

For more information:
Callaway Gardens
P.O. Box 2000
Pine Mountain, GA 31822-2000
(800) 225–5292
www.callawaygardens.com

10

Legends and Beauty Abound in Tallulah Gorge

Tallulah Gorge, one of the oldest gorges in North America, is best visited during spring water release, when the sights and sounds of rushing water are accented by the wildflowers adorning the gorge's rim.

Recommended time: Early April.

Name and location of site: Tallulah Gorge, immediately adjacent to the town of Tallulah Gorge.

Minimum time commitment: Two to four hours.

What to bring: Hiking shoes, binoculars, camera.

Admission fee: Daily parking $2.00 per vehicle; an annual Georgia ParkPass is $25. Discounts are available for senior citizens.

Directions: From the town of Tallulah Falls, travel northeast on I–85 for 18 miles to the junction of I–985. Veer to the left on I–985 and drive 13 miles to where I–985 turns into US 441. Continue on US 441 for 27 miles to the junction of US 441 across the bridge spanning the Tallulah River. Turn right on Jane Hurt Yarn Drive and drive to the Jane Hurt Yarn Interpretive Center.

The background: Tallulah Gorge is located in the 3,000-acre Tallulah Gorge State Park. The gorge is truly impressive, being more than 2 miles long and 1,000 feet deep at its deepest point. It was formed millions of years ago when the raging water of the Tallulah River carved a giant cleft in the earth

The Jane Hurt Yarn Interpretive Center, on the rim of Tallulah Gorge

on its headlong race to the sea. In the gorge, the waters of the Tallulah River drop nearly 600 feet in approximately a mile.

This area has captivated the imagination of all who have seen it. The Cherokees believed that the entrance to the Happy Hunting Grounds, an afterlife paradise where warriors would spend eternity happily hunting and eating, was hidden in a cave within the gorge. Their legends also spoke of little people that lived along the cliffs of the spectacular gorge.

During the 1800s, tourists from throughout the world flocked to the gorge to gaze at the water rushing over six impressive falls ranging in height from 16 to 98 feet. The sound made by the cascading water is said to have been deafening and could be heard for miles around.

Early in the twentieth century, the waters were diverted away from the falls through a tunnel almost 1.5 miles long and then through generators to produce electricity. Today the sounds of white water can only be heard during white-water boating and aesthetic water releases. The aesthetic releases (200 cubic feet per second) take place during the spring and fall. Visitors should call the park for the dates of these flows. White-water boating releases (500 cubic feet per second) are scheduled during the first two weekends of April and the first three weekends in November (from 8:00 A.M. to 4:00 P.M.). Kayakers are allowed to boat the river during the white-water releases, and kayaking is limited to 120 kayakers per weekend. The only access into the gorge at these times is through guided hikes. Call the park office for details.

Amazingly, two men have walked across the gorge on tightropes. Professor Leon was the first aerialist to accomplish this feat in 1886, and the last was Carl Wallenda, in 1970.

Tallulah Gorge is home to a wide array of wildlife and plants. Two of the rarer species that inhabit the gorge are the persistent trillium and green salamander.

The park has six hiking trails that range from moderate to difficult. Trails leading down into the gorge require free permits.

The Jane Hurt Yarn Interpretive Center sits near the north rim of the park. This 16,000-square-foot facility houses displays that interpret the geological, historical, cultural, and natural history of the area.

The fun: While a trip to Tallulah Gorge is always exciting, arguably the best times to go are during the times that water is released through the dam near the head of the gorge. On these occasions, the sights and sounds of water rushing down the rocky bed of the Tallulah River add a special dimension to the gorge. The spring is a particularly great time to experience a water release. Besides being a wonderful time of year to be outside, the wildflowers growing along the rim of the gorge add immeasurably to the outing.

When you arrive at the Jane Hurt Yarn Interpretive Center, spend some time looking at the interpretive displays. They will give you insights into what you are going to see and hear in the park.

Next, pick up a map and talk to an interpretive specialist about viewing opportunities as well as the length and difficulty of the hiking trails. Although there are many excellent places to view the gorge, some may be too far for you and your family to hike.

One of the best overlooks is the Hawthorne Overlook, which is only 0.2 mile down the North Rim Trail from the interpretive center. If you want to watch kayakers braving the white water of the Tallulah River below Hurricane Falls, you will have to trek west to Overlook 1. This vantage point is at the extreme eastern end of the North Rim Trail. The gorge is 750 feet deep at this point.

The complexion of the gorge changes throughout the day as the sun rises and sets over this natural wonder. For this reason, viewing the gorge from different vantage points on both the north and south rims at various times of the day gives viewers breathtaking panoramas. The images created by light and shadow are a photographer's dream.

Bring a picnic basket on your adventure. In the Day Use Area, visitors can dine at one of sixty-three picnic tables. This area also offers mountain biking, tennis and swimming in Tallulah Lake.

Food and lodging: There are fifty tent, trailer, and RV sites in the park. More than a dozen motels and bed-and-breakfast establishments and a dozen restaurants can be found within 15 miles of the gorge.

For more information:

Tallulah Gorge State Park
P.O. Box 248
Tallulah Falls, GA 30573
(706) 754–7970 (office) or (706) 754–7979 (camping)

11

Spring

Battlefield Songsters

Warblers in vibrant spring colors use this stopover spot to rest and refuel during migration.

Recommended time: Late April through early May.

Name and location of site: Kennesaw Mountain National Battlefield, 13 miles (fifteen minutes) northwest of Atlanta.

Minimum time commitment: Three to four hours.

What to bring: Good walking shoes, binoculars, a field guide to birds, camera.

Admission fee: None.

Directions: In Marietta, at the junction of I–75 (exit 269) and SR 5C, turn left onto SR 5C (Barrett Parkway) and continue 2.2 miles to the intersection of SR 5C and Old US 41. Turn left on Old US 41 and travel 1.4 miles, and then turn right onto Stilesboro Road. You will see the entrance to the park on your left.

The background: Bird migration is one of the most spectacular events in the natural world. Twice yearly millions of birds fly hundreds, even thousands, of miles from their nesting grounds throughout North America to wintering areas in such foreign ports of call as the Caribbean islands, Mexico, and Central and South America. It is difficult for us to comprehend the magnitude of this event since nothing in our lives remotely compares to this biannual passage.

Some 340 species of birds that nest in North America migrate. Many of these birds, such as juncos and wood ducks, often migrate only a few hundred miles annually. More than one hundred species of birds, like the scarlet tanager and hooded warbler, however, primarily winter south of U.S. borders.

Most birds cannot carry enough fuel, in the form of fat, to fly nonstop between their wintering and nesting grounds. Consequently, they must stop at sites, called stopover areas, to rest and refuel before continuing on their way.

One of the best-known places in the Southeast to observe migrating songbirds is at the stopover site of Kennesaw Mountain. The mountain soars 1,000 feet above the urban sprawl that surrounds Atlanta. Here tired and hungry migrants find a bounty of food and a place to rest in the hardwood forest that blankets the mountain.

This important stopover area is used by thirty-five species of warblers alone. The spring warbler migration at Kennesaw Mountain that begins in mid-March is over by May 30 with the peak coming from the third weekend in April to the first weekend in May. During the peak of this migration it is not uncommon to see twenty or more species of warblers on a trek up the mountain. On a really good morning, up to thirty species can be sighted.

Warblers are small (usually 5 to 6 inches long), insect-eating (insectivorous) birds that nest throughout most of North America. They are among the most colorful birds found in the New World. These birds, called wood warblers by ornithologists, are most beautiful in the spring. During this season their vibrant colors make the birds look like brightly colored jewels as they forage for insects in the fresh green foliage.

Kennesaw Mountain sits amid the Kennesaw Mountain National Battlefield. This beautiful 2,800-acre area was set aside to preserve an important Civil War battlefield. In 1864, thousands of men from both the North and the South lost their lives here as the Confederate Army vainly tried to stop Gen. William Tecumseh Sherman's march toward the city of Atlanta.

Each year the battlefield hosts 1.3 million visitors that come here to learn more about this famous battle as well as to jog, bird-watch, and picnic. On weekends during the peak of bird migration, bird-watchers are among the primary users of the area.

The fun: You will want to get an early start on this trip since some of the best birding takes place during the first few hours after daylight.

While there are 16 miles of trails in the area, most bird-watching is done along the 1.2-mile paved road that winds its way to the top of the mountain. During the week the road is open for vehicular traffic. However, on weekends

Not So Common Anymore

After spending a morning watching scarlet tanagers, hooded and cerulean warblers, and a host of other colorful migrants feeding in the lush foliage on the slopes of Kennesaw Mountain, it is easy to believe that all is well with our songbirds. However, the populations of many of these beautiful songsters are steadily dwindling. This is particularly true of many members of a group of birds called neotropical migrants.

Neotropical migrants are birds that nest in North America and winter in the Caribbean, Mexico, and Central and South America. They include most of the warblers, tanagers, vireos, thrushes, orioles, and flycatchers, to name a few.

In the ten-year period from 1980 to 1989, 53 percent of the neotropical migrants that nest in Georgia declined in population. In comparison, neotropical migrants nesting in Vermont suffered an 85 percent population decline during the same time period. The list of birds whose populations are plummeting includes the yellow-billed cuckoo, scarlet tanager, wood thrush, ovenbird, American redstart, black-throated blue warbler, magnolia warbler, great-crested flycatcher, and many others.

Biologists believe that there are many reasons for the population declines of many of our neotropical migrants. Habitat loss is thought to play a key role in these declines. Habitat loss is taking place where the birds nest, where they stop on migration, and on their wintering grounds as well.

Each year, more and more forests and other wildlife habitats are being lost to housing developments, roads, shopping centers, and agricultural land. Other forested tracts are being converted from hardwoods to fast-growing pines.

Habitat fragmentation is also a problem. Some birds, such as the wood thrush, need large tracts of forest for nesting. When these forests are cut into small tracts, nesting thrushes are vulnerable to nest predators, such as cats and blue jays, and parasites like the brown-headed cowbird, which doesn't build its own nest. Instead, female cowbirds lay their eggs in the nests of other birds. These eggs usually hatch before the other eggs in the nest. Since the young cowbirds grow quickly, their adopted parents often end up spending most of their time feeding them instead of their own young. This often results in the parents raising cowbirds instead of their own offspring.

Another real problem is the destruction of habitat in the tropics. Our Latin American neighbors are logging their forests or converting the lands to pastures or farmland devoted to sun-grown coffee, bananas, and other crops at an unprecedented rate. As a result, many of our neotropical migrants are having difficulty finding suitable wintering habitats.

Private and government conservation groups that are concerned about the plight of our neotropical migrants have banded together to form an organization called Partners In Flight. The alliance has launched a number of education, habitat management, research, and survey initiatives that are designed to stem the declines in our neotropical migrants. If you would like to learn how you can help Partners In Flight "keep common birds common," contact your state's wildlife agency.

the only vehicle allowed on the road is a park bus that transports guests to the top of the mountain and back for a small fee. The bus runs every half hour, beginning at 9:30 A.M.

If you are a beginner who wants to learn about birds, plan your trip for a Saturday. Each Saturday during the spring migration, the Atlanta Audubon Society holds field trips at the battlefield. These trips are open to both members and guests alike. The more experienced birders on these trips enjoy acting as mentors to those wanting to hone their bird-identification skills. Weather permitting, the walks begin at the far end of the parking lot at 7:30 A.M.

If you want to strike out on your own, begin your search by walking around the parking lot. It is surprising how many birds can be seen here, especially before the crowds begin to arrive later in the morning.

When you are ready to make your ascent up the mountain, you must choose between two routes. While the Mountaintop Trail offers a more traditional hiking experience, most people opt for walking the road. The walk up the mountain is strenuous. Regardless of which route you pick, take your time, and stop frequently to look for birds. Plenty of birds can be seen without having to go all the way to the top.

If you do trek to the top of the mountain, you are rewarded with a great view of Atlanta. On a clear day, Stone Mountain can be seen in the distance.

As you make your way uphill, you are eye level with much of the tree canopy on the downhill side of the road. Since many warblers feed in the tops of trees, you can easily view their colorful plumage from the side. This allows for easier identification and appreciation of their natural beauty. Don't forget to look for birds on the uphill side of the road. Some warblers, such as the ovenbird, prefer to feed near the ground.

When you see groups with their binoculars pointed in the same direction, this is a good indication that they have made an interesting discovery. People will enthusiastically help you to locate birds that they have found.

If you don't want to confine your birding to the road, walk down one of the several trails that intersect the road. If you decide to explore some of these trails, watch out for hikers and joggers. On busy weekends birders have to share these narrow pathways.

While warblers are the main attraction, you will also see a variety of other fascinating birds, such as thrushes, vireos, and tanagers. From the overlooks hawks and eagles can be seen.

The memorials, cannon, and other relics are reminders of the bloody battle that was waged on these lands more than a century ago. Today it is comforting to see that the scars of war on the landscape have healed and that those scaling the hillside are armed with binoculars instead of rifles.

Food and lodging: More than two dozen restaurants and four motels can be found within 2 miles of the park.

For more information:
Kennesaw Mountain National Battlefield
900 Kennesaw Mountain Drive
Kennesaw, GA 30144
(470) 427–4686
or
Atlanta Audubon Society
Box 29189
Atlanta, GA 30359
(770) 955–4111

12

Spring

A Hubbub of Nesting Activity

When you blend patience and time, you can observe the daily chores at a wood-stork rookery.

Recommended time: April.

Name and location of site: Harris Neck National Wildlife Refuge, less than 10 miles from South Newport.

Minimum time commitment: Two hours.

What to bring: Binoculars, spotting scope, field guide to birds, insect repellent, and folding chairs.

Admission fee: None.

Directions: Just north of the town of South Newport, at the junction of I–95 (exit 67) and US 17, turn onto US 17 and drive south for 1.2 miles to the junction of Harris Neck Road (CR 246), just past the Smallest Church in America. Turn left onto Harris Neck Road and continue 7.4 miles to the refuge entrance. Turn left into the refuge and proceed to the beginning of the wildlife driving trail (first road on the right). Continue down the driving trail to the parking area near Woody Pond.

The background: The wood stork is the only true stork that nests in North America. Wood storks breed from the southeastern United States southward into Mexico, Cuba, and Central and South America. In Georgia they're known to breed in only thirteen counties, found in extreme south Georgia and along the coast.

Biologists estimate that as many as 20,000 pairs of wood storks nested in the United States during the 1930s. However, by the late 1970s the American breeding population had plummeted to between 4,500 and 5,700 pairs. The precipitous decline in wood stork populations resulted in this long-legged wader being listed as endangered on both the Federal Endangered Species List and the Georgia Protected Species List.

One of the few places where wood storks can be easily viewed while they are nesting is at the 2,763-acre Harris Neck National Wildlife Refuge. The refuge occupies the site of an abandoned U.S. Army Air Force Base. During World War II airplanes stationed at the base defended the Georgia coast from German submarines that plied the waters close to shore. Today the refuge is home to an amazing array of wildlife, such as white-tailed deer, songbirds, wading birds, waterfowl, and others.

The refuge is ideally suited for wildlife-watching, with 15 miles of paved roads crisscrossing the area. The highlight of this road network is a 4-mile wildlife drive.

The fun: This adventure takes place on the dam that impounds Woody Pond. After you have parked your car, walk out onto the dam. Woody Pond will be on your left. The wood storks will be nesting at the far end of the impoundment.

While you will be able to see the birds through binoculars, a spotting scope can be an advantage on this trip. It will permit you to discern details of the birds and their behavior that are difficult with binoculars alone.

On most days, Woody Pond is alive with wildlife. There will be many wading birds present. In spite of this, the wood stork should be quite easy to identify as it has a unique color pattern. The wood stork stands about 3 feet tall and has a 5-foot wingspan. It has black legs and pink toes. Its bill is long and down-curved. Its body feathers are white; its wing tips, trailing edges of its wings, and tail are black. The wood stork's head and neck are dark and lack feathers.

The center of their activity will be the artificial nesting structures that stand above the water. These unique nesting sites are nothing more than shallow wire baskets mounted on crosspieces bolted to tall poles erected in the pond. These innovative nesting structures were placed here because the existing trees could not support a wood-stork nesting colony.

Depending on when you visit the site, you may see birds incubating eggs or feeding young, or the young standing up in the nest, waiting for their parents to bring them food.

When young are in the nest, the adults will feed them about twelve times

Wood storks nest on artificial nesting structures.

a day. Wood storks will be coming to or leaving the colony throughout the day. When a parent arrives at the nest, it will not be carrying food in its bill. The adults swallow their prey when they catch it. When they get to the nest, the food is regurgitated at the feet of their hungry young.

Don't be surprised if you see some storks flying into the rookery carrying sticks. Wood storks will often add sticks to their crude nests after their young hatch. After seeing their nests, you will understand why the parents probably need to make nest repairs from time to time.

Another interesting behavior to look for is an adult shading its young. During the youngsters' first five weeks of life, one of the adults will stay at the nest to offer some protection against the blazing hot sun.

These are just a few of the fascinating things that can be seen going on in a wood-stork rookery. When you blend patience and time, you have all of the makings for a wildlife adventure that you will long remember.

Food and lodging: A restaurant and an RV park can be found at exit 67 off I–95.

For more information:
U. S. Fish and Wildlife Service
Savannah Coastal Refuges
1000 Business Center Drive
Parkway Business Center, Suite 10
Savannah, GA 31405
(912) 652–4415

13

Spring

The Swamp Canary

A beautiful river swamp is home to one of Georgia's most beautiful, but seldom seen, birds, the prothonotary warbler.

Recommended time: 9:00 A.M. to 5:00 P.M. any weekend in April and May.

Name and location of site: Savannah-Ogeechee Canal Museum and Nature Center, 7.9 miles (ten minutes) south of the junction of I–16 and I–95, west of Savannah.

Minimum time commitment: One to two hours.

What to bring: Camera; field guides to birds, plants, and reptiles and amphibians; insect repellent.

Admission fee: Children five and under, free; students and senior citizens, $1.00; adults, $2.00.

Directions: From Savannah: From the junction of I–16 and I–95, take I–95 South (5.6 miles) to the junction of SR 204 (exit 94). Turn right on SR 204 and travel 2.3 miles west to the Savannah-Ogeechee Canal Museum and Nature Center, which will be on your left.

The background: A visit to the Savannah-Ogeechee Canal Museum and Nature Center gives the visitor the unique opportunity to comfortably trek back into a lush, tidal river swamp along the towpaths that hug the sides of the once prosperous Savannah-Ogeechee Canal. The canal, built in 1830, was used for decades to transport timber, rice, cotton, naval stores, and other goods. Throughout much of the nineteenth century, the song of the prothonotary warbler, sometimes called the swamp canary, competed with the sounds of commerce. Today the prothonotary warbler and other denizens of the swamp live out their lives along the crumbling remains of what was once a vital artery of commerce.

The museum and nature center sits on a 184-acre tract. Most of the area is located in the Ogeechee River floodplain; however, the site also has some pine flatwoods and sandhill habitats. These habitats are home to an impressive array of plants and animals, including the bright yellow prothonotary warbler—one of the most handsome birds in Georgia. This beautiful, sparrow-size summer resident is easy to identify. Male prothonotary warblers sport a bright orange-yellow head and breast. The bird's back is olive, while its wings are blue gray. The female and young are duller versions of the male.

Eighty-eight species of reptiles and amphibians are found here, including the gopher tortoise, scarlet kingsnake, barking treefrog, slender glass lizard, and southern red salamander. White-tailed deer, armadillos, and raccoons roam the uplands. Beavers and otters patrol the water courses. Scores of birds can be seen here, including the wood duck, Swainson's warbler, summer tanager, great egret, and barred owl. A variety of oak, cypress, pignut hickory, southern magnolia, and other trees form a living umbrella over a moist forest floor where scattered stands of ferns abound.

The fun: Begin your adventure with a visit to the small museum. A few minutes spent looking at the displays will give you a quick overview of the human and natural history of the area. You are now ready to enter the swamp. There are six short trails that lead to various areas on the site. Begin by walking the Tow Path Trail, which runs along the east side of the canal. This trail is only 0.4 mile long and ends where the canal joins the Ogeechee River. You can best enjoy your trek down this path by moving at a slow pace. There is so much to see and hear as you make your way toward the Ogeechee River.

This is a great time of year to find the prothonotary warbler. In early April, soon after the males arrive from their wintering grounds in Central America and northwestern South America, they begin to set up breeding territories. Throughout the nesting season they incessantly utter their sweet-sounding *zweet, zweet, zweet, zweet, zweet, zweet* calls. These calls are often made from high in a tree. The males also have a canary-like song that they make while flying.

These vocalizations can be extremely helpful when trying to find the birds in the thick foliage. Prothonotary warblers can also be spotted when they are not calling; look for them feeding on insects and snails near the water or in low shrubs.

Seeing your first prothonotary warbler is an unforgettable experience. Its

The old barge towpath provides easy access to the Ogeechee River Swamp.

bright yellow feathers seem to possess an inner glow when contrasted against the black water of the swamp and the dark green foliage. After seeing this yellow bird, you can understand why it's also called the swamp canary.

The prothonotary warbler is the only eastern warbler that nests in cavities. Carefully watch any tree cavities that you might find. Should you spot the warblers using a cavity, you are in for a real treat. If a male is seen carrying Spanish moss to a hole in a tree, he is not helping build a nest that will cradle a clutch of eggs—he is making a dummy nest in hopes of attracting a female. Only females construct the nests. Should the cavity contain young prothonotary warblers, you will be able to see both parents bringing food to their nestlings.

After walking the Tow Path Trail, take the time to walk some of the other trails. Each trail has its own special features.

Food and lodging: Numerous motels and restaurants can be found in nearby Savannah.

For more information:
Savannah-Ogeechee Canal Museum and Nature Center
681 Fort Argyle Road
Savannah, GA 31419-9239
(912) 748-8068

14

Spring

A Torrent of Shoals Spiderlilies

*Take in the fleeting sight and scent of the rare and beautiful shoals
spiderlily blooming above the moving waters of Big Lazer Creek.*

Recommended time: Mid- to late May.

Name and location of site: Big Lazer Creek Wildlife Management
Area, approximately 15 miles from Thomaston.

Minimum time commitment: One hour.

What to bring: Binoculars, field guide to wildflowers, camera, insect
repellent.

Admission fee: None.

Directions: From Thomaston travel south 4 miles on US 19 to the junction of Po Biddy Road. Turn right on Po Biddy Road and continue 11 miles
to the junction of Bunkham Road. Look for the Big Lazer Creek Wildlife
Management Area sign on the left. Turn right down Bunkham Road and
drive north. The Big Lazer Creek Checking Station (on the left) is located
1.5 miles down Bunkham Road; continue on across the dam to River Road.
River Road is 1.7 miles from the Checking Station. At this intersection, a
camping area is located on the right side of the road. Turn right on River
Road and proceed 2.8 miles to the end of the road near the river. Park your
vehicle and walk to the river.

The background: While the shoals spiderlily is one of the most stun-
ningly beautiful native plants found in Georgia, its ephemeral beauty is rarely
enjoyed by most outdoor enthusiasts. Although it ranges across the states of

Alabama, South Carolina, and Georgia, it is rare wherever it grows and has been found in only eighteen streams throughout its range. In the Peach State, it grows in only five streams spread across eight counties. Consequently, it is listed as endangered on Georgia's Protected Species List. The plant is also a candidate for listing on the Federal Endangered Species List.

One reason for its scarcity is that the shoals spiderlily has very specific habitat requirements. It grows in the rocky shoals of unpolluted streams rich in dissolved oxygen and not plagued with high siltation. Increased pollution, poor land management practices, and the impoundment of free-flowing streams have all greatly reduced the places where this rare wildflower can grow.

The shoals spiderlily blooms above the rushing waters of the Flint River.

In April shoals spiderlily plants can be seen poking above the surface of the water. By mid-May they are ready to bloom. These plants sprout from bulbs that are wedged between the cracks and crevices in the shoals.

By the time the plants are ready to bloom, they are more than 3 feet tall. Each plant sends up one to three stalks that bear six to nine flowers each. These stunning white flowers have yellow centers and measure about 6 inches across. Each individual flower has a fleeting existence: It will open in late afternoon only to shrivel before sunset on the following day. Customarily only a single flower blooms on a stalk at a time.

While the delicate flower is blooming, it emits a pleasing aroma. This scent attracts nocturnal pollinators such as the plebian sphinx moth. This moth is well adapted for this task, having a proboscis that measures more than 2 inches long. This allows the moth to reach the sugary nectar found at the base of the flower's long throat.

Shoals spiderlilies (sometimes called cahaba lilies) bloom in Georgia from mid-May to early June. This stand is particularly showy around May 20.

The fun: Your destination is the Big Lazer Creek Wildlife Management Area. Here at the confluence of Big Lazer Creek and the Flint River, you will see one of the best stands of shoals spiderlilies found in Georgia. If you visit this site at the right time, you can gaze upon thousands of gorgeous lilies blooming above the moving water. The combination of the sound of flowing waters and the sight of white flowers accented by the dark rocks of the shoal will leave an indelible image in your mind. Bring your camera as you will want a photographic record of this natural spectacle. Don't forget, blooms don't begin to open until late afternoon.

When you gaze across this indescribable scene, you might feel the urge to take home some of these showy plants. Don't do it. It is illegal to pick or dig up these state-protected plants. In some parts of its range, shoals spiderlily populations have been decimated by uncaring individuals that thought they could raise these plants at home. Shoals spiderlilies have very specific habitat requirements that cannot be matched in a backyard or stream on your property. By viewing and not destroying these plants, we can help ensure that they will be there to enjoy for many springs to come.

Food and lodging: Six motels and more than twenty restaurants can be found in nearby Thomaston.

For more information:
Wildlife Resources Division
Game Management Section
1014 Martin Luther King Boulevard
Fort Valley, GA 31030
(478) 825–6354

15

Spring

The Magnolia Wedding Chapel

A landmark tree in many ways, this magnificent magnolia has amazed generations of Georgians.

Recommended time: Late spring or early summer.

Name and location of site: The Tift Magnolia Tree, 1.5 miles east of I–75 in Tifton.

Minimum time commitment: One hour.

What to bring: Camera.

Admission fee: None.

Directions: In Tifton, at the junction of I–75 (exit 59) and Southwell Road, travel east on Southwell Road for 0.8 mile to the junction of Magnolia Industrial Boulevard. Turn right on Magnolia Industrial Boulevard. The tree is located 0.7 mile farther on the right.

The background: The Tift Magnolia Tree is truly an impressive sight. While other southern magnolias *(Magnolia grandifolia)* may stand taller than this tree's 69 feet, few, if any, can match its crown spread, which stretches 105 feet. Its massive trunk's circumference is 69 feet.

The southern magnolia, or bull bay, is a tree common to the Coastal Plain region of the southeastern United States. It is usually found growing in swamps and along stream courses. It has also been widely introduced to other areas of the South.

This evergreen tree bears long leathery leaves that measure from 5 to 10 inches long. These leaves are typically shiny and bright green on top with undersides that are usually hairy and rusty in color.

During the late spring and early summer, magnolia trees are festooned with large (7 to 8 inches in diameter) fragrant flowers. Fruits are cone shaped and packed with red berries. Turkey, quail, and other seed-eating animals eat the berries.

The Magnolia Tree Association estimates that the Tift Magnolia Tree sprouted about 400 years ago, approximately one hundred years before the birth of the founder of Georgia, Gen. James Edward Oglethorpe.

Over the years, the tree has been used in many ways. At one time, its massive spreading branches were used to protect farm equipment from the elements. Couples have even been joined in holy matrimony in this leafy bower. In addition, generations of Georgians have enjoyed its beauty and form. Today this natural wonder grows in a park a short distance off I–75. The tree even has a foundation that looks after its health and safety.

In 1995 this special tree was dubbed a landmark tree in the Georgia Landmark and Historic Tree Register.

The fun: The best time to visit the Tift Magnolia Tree is while it is blooming. At that time of year, thousands of saucer-size blooms adorn the tree and fill the air with their lemony scent. The sight and scent of this natural event assault the senses.

The tree sits in a fenced, grassy park alongside a road (Magnolia Boulevard) named in its honor. Picnic tables are provided for travelers wishing to dine near this majestic tree.

Two barrier-free ramps and platforms allow visitors the opportunity to easily view the tree from beneath its branches. On a hot day, temperatures beneath the canopy of the tree are ten to fifteen degrees cooler than outside.

Food and lodging: More than three dozen restaurants and a dozen motels are located in Tifton.

For more information:
The Magnolia Tree Foundation
P.O. Box 1803
Tifton, GA 31794
or
Tifton–Tift County Chamber of Commerce
P.O. Box 165
Tifton, GA 31793
(229) 382–6200

16

A Walk Back in Time

The record of the events that formed this picturesque landscape is written in layers of rock deposited at the bottom of an ancient sea.

Recommended time: May.

Name and location of site: Cloudland Canyon State Park, 109 miles (2 hours) northwest of Atlanta.

Minimum time commitment: Three to four hours.

What to bring: Camera, binoculars, comfortable hiking shoes.

Admission fee: Daily parking is $2.00 per vehicle; an annual Georgia ParkPass is $25. Discounts are available for senior citizens.

Directions: From LaFayette, at the junction of SR 136 and US 27, travel north on US 27 for 3 miles to the junction of US 27 and SR 136. Turn left on SR 136 and drive 17 miles to the park entrance.

The background: Cloudland Canyon, often called the Grand Canyon of north Georgia, is one of the most beautiful canyons found in the Southeast. At its deepest point, this Y-shaped canyon measures 1,000 feet from its rim to the canyon floor. A visitor making the steep descent into the canyon is provided with arguably the finest opportunity to study the geology of northwest Georgia.

Geologists tell us that 250 to 310 million years ago, the land where the canyon now sits was at the bottom of the sea. Over millions of years the sea slowly receded to the point where the top of the current canyon was an ancient beach. For the past thirty million years, Sitton Gulch Creek has been inexorably eroding away at the sedimentary rocks found here.

Interestingly, the canyon was the last place where peregrine falcons nested in Georgia before the Georgia Wildlife Resources Division began efforts to reintroduce this magnificent bird to the state during the 1980s. A nest was found on one of the canyon's sandstone cliffs in 1942.

Cloudland Canyon is the centerpiece of the 2,219-acre Cloudland Canyon State Park. Tucked in the northwest corner of the state, the park is a favorite destination for outdoor recreationists.

The fun: Begin your adventure with a stop at the Cloudland Canyon State Park Office. The park employees are an invaluable source of information regarding both the natural and geologic history of the park. Besides the free literature offered by the park, visitors can purchase guidebooks that can be a tremendous help in simply knowing what you are looking at. Don Pfitzer's *Hiking Georgia* contains a wealth of detailed information about what hikers will encounter as they trek around and into the canyon. The literature supplements the excellent interpretive information that you will find throughout the park. Being able to spot and understand the fascinating geologic features that you will find on your descent into the canyon can add immeasurably to your experience.

Next, drive to the parking lot that services the West Rim Overlook and Picnic Area. The trailhead for the trail leading into the canyon is located nearby. While it is a short hike into the canyon, this trail is quite steep and strenuous. If you decide to go down into the canyon, you will be richly rewarded for your efforts. The natural beauty that surrounds this picturesque trail assails the senses. If that isn't enough, at the bottom of the canyon you will find two superb waterfalls. The upper falls is created by water rushing over a bowl-shaped rock before falling 50 feet into a pool. The lower falls is the taller of the two. Here water tumbles 90 feet before continuing its journey out of the canyon.

If you prefer to view this canyon from the rim, visit the overlooks strategically placed around the park. Bring your camera and plenty of film as you will want to preserve scenes of this natural wonderland.

Spring is a great time of year to visit the park. Blooming wildflowers festoon the sides of the trails. In addition, the waterfalls are exceptionally beautiful as the volume of water flowing over the two waterfalls is usually greatest at this time of the year.

Food and lodging: Travelers will find seventy-five tent, trailer, and RV

The geologic history of the canyon is written on its rocky cliffs.

sites; sixteen cottages; and four pioneer campgrounds (only available to groups; includes facilities of tent sites and primitive privies) within the park. In addition, one motel and ten restaurants are within 5 miles of the park.

For more information:
Cloudland Canyon State Park
Route 2, Box 150
Rising Fawn, GA 30738
(706) 657–4050

17

Spring

In Quest of Georgia's Most Beautiful Bird

This Civil War site, steeped in history, offers wildlife a safe haven and wildlife watchers a closer look at the vibrant painted bunting and other wild residents.

Recommended time: Mid-April to mid-September.

Name and location of site: Fort Pulaski National Monument, approximately 13 miles east of Savannah.

Minimum time commitment: One to two hours.

What to bring: Binoculars, field guide to birds, insect repellent, sunscreen.

Admission fee: None to enter the grounds, but there is a fee to tour the historical site.

Directions: In Savannah, at the junction of I–16 (exit 165) and SR 204, turn right onto SR 204 and continue south 1.7 miles to US 80. Make a left-hand turn onto US 80. Head east 13.3 miles to the entrance (on left) to Fort Pulaski.

The background: The Fort Pulaski National Monument is situated at the mouth of the Savannah River on 5,365 acres of salt marsh and island habitats. Fort Pulaski, completed in 1847, was built to protect the port of Savannah from foreign attack. The fort is named for Count Casimir Pulaski, a hero of the Revolutionary War who was killed in a siege of Savannah in 1779. When the fort's 7.5-foot-thick brick walls were built, military experts felt that they were unbreachable.

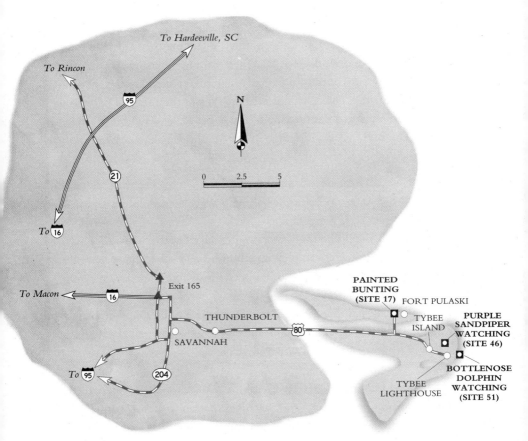

During the early stages of the Civil War, Fort Pulaski was seized by the Georgia Militia in 1861 only a week after federal troops had taken over Fort Sumter. Then, in 1862, after thirty hours of bombardment from Union troops on nearby Tybee Island, the Confederate forces surrendered the fort. The "impregnable" walls of the fort had been breached by the rifled artillery of the Union. Today visitors can tour this well-preserved national monument and see the damage inflicted on Fort Pulaski by the bullet-shaped projectiles that changed the warfare of the times.

Since the Civil War, nature has been slowly changing the landscape of this historical site. One species that has benefited from these changes is the painted bunting. Like many of our migratory songbirds, painted bunting populations are plummeting. However, here at Fort Pulaski they are still commonly found. The male painted bunting sports a blue head, and a red breast, chest, and rump. The bird's back and wings are green. The female is cloaked in drab green.

The fun: As you turn off US 80 onto the entrance road to the fort, take a close look at the water on both sides of the bridge. Both dolphins and manatees are sometimes seen here.

Your first stop should be the visitors center adjacent to the parking lot in front of the fort. Here you can pick up a bird list and other interpretive materials. The park rangers can also direct you to where they have recently seen painted buntings.

The monument has three trails. The dike trail is 2 miles long, the picnic area trail measures 0.5 mile in length, and the accessibility trail is only 0.25 mile long. The accessibility trail is paved, while the other two trails are unpaved.

The painted bunting is a secretive bird that likes to feed at or near the ground in or near brushy areas and the edges of woods. Consequently, if it were not for the fact that the male sings from the time it arrives here until late summer, it would be extremely difficult to find. Male painted buntings like to sing from high perches. Look for them near the tops of trees and on utility lines. Slowly walk the nature trails and the edge of the open areas around the fort looking and listening for the bird. The male's song is a sweet, musical warble. Its call is an abrupt *chit*.

Before embarking on any of the trails, spray yourself with insect repellent. Biting and stinging insects can sometimes be a problem here.

During the spring and fall migrations, the area is a haven for bird-watchers. More than two dozen warblers and five species of thrushes have been reported

Visitors to Fort Pulaski can enjoy both natural and human history.

in the thickets and woods of the fort. Clapper rails can be seen and heard in the marsh throughout the year. Shorebirds, gulls, terns, and wading birds can be spotted from the dike trail. Some of the mammals that you might see include otter, mink, raccoon, gray fox, and bobcat.

After you have completed your quest for the painted bunting, take time to visit the visitors center and Fort Pulaski. Park rangers and interpretive exhibits do an excellent job of interpreting the human history of this nineteenth-century fort.

The fort is open from 8:30 A.M. to 5:15 P.M. daily. The visitors center is open from 8:30 A.M. to 5:00 P.M.

Food and lodging: Scores of motels and restaurants can be found within thirty minutes of the site on Tybee Island and in Savannah.

For more information:

Superintendent
Fort Pulaski National Monument
P.O. Box 30757
Savannah, GA 31410-0757
(912) 786–5787

18

Summer

Shady Pools and Monster Trout

Deep, clear pools on Dukes Creek make for exceptional viewing of brook, brown, and rainbow trout.

Recommended time: July through August.

Name and location of site: Smithgall Woods–Dukes Creek Conservation Area, just a few miles from Helen.

Minimum time commitment: One to two hours.

What to bring: Binoculars, polarized sunglasses

Admission fee: Daily parking is $2.00 per vehicle; an annual Georgia ParkPass is $25. Discounts are available for senior citizens.

Directions: From Helen travel north 1 mile to the junction of SR 75 and SR 75A. Turn left on SR 75A and continue for 2 miles to the Smithgall Woods entrance sign.

The background: Trout are highly prized by anglers. In Georgia trout are found only in the northern portion of the state, living in streams where water temperatures don't exceed 70 degrees Fahrenheit. While wildlife watchers are also interested in these game fish, aside from fish hatcheries there are few places where they can be viewed. Dukes Creek, rated by Trout Unlimited as one of the Top 100 Trout Streams in the United States, provides an ideal setting to see big trout in the wild. Here the creek's deep, clear, shaded pools abound with trout. These fish average 19 to 20 inches long, with some lunkers measuring up to 28 inches long.

The Smithgall Woods–Dukes Creek Conservation area is managed by the

Georgia Department of Natural Resources. This 5,604-acre tract was acquired in 1994 and has been designated as a Heritage Preserve.

Dukes Creek is liberally stocked with trout to give anglers an outstanding opportunity to catch large trout. The periodic stockings also enhance the chances that visitors can see trout in a natural setting. Dukes Creek is a catch-and-release stream. Here anglers are required to use artificial lures equipped with barbless hooks. This makes the fishing experience more sporting and heightens the chances that the fish released will live to fight another day.

Three species of trout swim the waters of Dukes Creek. The two most common trout are browns and rainbows. Lesser numbers of brook trout also inhabit the creek. The brook trout is the only species of trout native to Georgia. Once they were found in streams large and small throughout the Georgia mountains. Today native brook trout are found in a fraction of the waters where they once thrived. This, our smallest trout (rarely exceeding two pounds), has been displaced by both rainbow and brown trout. The brook trout's back and sides are olive brown to slate colored. Their sides are also adorned with red spots surrounded with blue halos. All of their fins, except the dorsal, have white borders. Their backs are marked with wormlike markings.

Trophy trout can be seen from a footbridge spanning Dukes Creek.

Rainbow trout were brought to the Georgia mountains decades ago by a famous pioneering forest ranger named Arthur Woody. Rainbows are native to the mountain streams of the western United States. While rainbow trout have been known to tip the scales at forty pounds, most rainbows weigh five pounds or less. The rainbow trout gets its name from the reddish stripe that extends down its sides. This trout also has a slightly forked tail and black spots on its body, as well as on its tail and dorsal fins.

The brown trout has a square, almost unspotted tail. Its body is olive brown and highlighted with red spots surrounded by blue halos. These spots are also present on the tail. The brown trout is our largest trout, weighing up to forty pounds; however, few ever reach more than five pounds. The brown trout is a native of northern Europe.

The fun: If the only trout watching you have ever done has been at a fish hatchery or aquarium, you are in for a unique experience. Nothing quite compares to watching trout in their natural environment. Here you can gain a better appreciation of how a fish's camouflage helps protect it from predators, learn its habitat preferences, watch as it uses its acute senses to detect danger and locate food, and see how its streamlined body makes it ideally suited to live in fast moving water.

Begin your adventure by visiting the visitors center. Here staff members can direct you to some of the best places to see trout. The center is open Monday, Tuesday, Thursday, and Friday from 8:00 A.M. to 4:00 P.M. and Wednesday, Saturday, and Sunday from half an hour before sunrise to half an hour after sunset.

While trout can be located practically anywhere in Dukes Creek, a good place to start looking for them is directly across the street from the visitors center's parking lot. A well-maintained footpath meanders along the edge of the stream. Follow the path toward its terminus near the highway. Cross the highway and follow the creek as it winds its way along a paved road toward the cabins.

The fish congregate in the deep pools scattered along the creek, waiting for food to be washed downstream into the lairs. The relatively calm surfaces of the pools allow you to peer deep into the water. Since the pools are, for the most part, shrouded in shadows, you will really have to look closely to see the trout. A pair of polarized sunglasses is a real asset in this type of wildlife watching. The glasses significantly cut down glare and allow the wearer to see fish that are not or barely visible to the naked eye. Similarly, if you are going to try to take pictures of the lunker trout, use a polarized filter on your camera lens.

These fish are extremely skittish. Approach the stream slowly, making sure that you don't cast any shadows on the water. It is also a good idea not to run or make loud noises near the streambank as this will alarm fish swimming nearby. If you find that the fish disappear at your approach, stand beside a tree or sit and wait. In a short while they should come out of hiding and resume their normal activities.

If you come across an angler, don't walk along the streambank in front of him. This courtesy will keep you from spooking fish that he or she is trying to catch.

After you finish your trout-watching expedition, you might want to take advantage of some of the other outdoor activities offered at this beautiful conservation area. Wednesday, Saturday, and Sunday, beginning at 9:00 A.M., shuttle tours are offered every two hours throughout the day. The tour passes through some of the most picturesque areas found on this haven for wild plants and animals. Since only eight to ten seats are available per tour, call ahead for a tour schedule and reservations.

Four trails are provided for hiking and nature study. The 1.5-mile Laurel Ridge Trail begins at the visitors center. The trailhead for the Cathy Ellis Trail is situated about 3 miles away. The Martin's Mine Trail (2.1 miles) is accessed off Shackleford Road. The trailhead for the Falls Trail (2.8 miles) is located on Tsalaki Trail, east of the junction of Shackleford Road.

Biking is allowed along the area's 12 miles of improved roads. Before embarking on a bike trip, make sure you pick up a biking permit at the visitors center. Picnicking is allowed in designated areas only.

Special programs dealing with a variety of natural history subjects are presented throughout the year. Call or write for a schedule of events.

Food and lodging: Limited lodging is available in the area. The Lodge at Smithgall has five cottages that can accommodate up to twenty-eight guests. Nightly rates include three meals per day. Groups can also stay at the area's Bear Ridge Group Camp. Travelers can find a wide selection of overnight accommodations and restaurants in nearby Helen.

For more information:
Smithgall Woods
61 Tsalaki Trail
Helen, GA 30545
(706) 878–3087

19

Summer

Butterflies Flutter in the Summer Sun

The Annual North American Butterfly Association's Fourth of July
Butterfly Count is for experts and beginners alike.

Recommended time: July.

Name and location of site: Harris Neck National Wildlife Refuge,
less than 10 miles from South Newport.

Minimum time commitment: Four hours.

What to bring: Field guide to butterflies, a pair of close-focusing binoculars, insect repellent, sunscreen.

Admission fee: $5.00 participation fee.

Directions: Just north of the town of South Newport at the junction of
I–95 (exit 67) and US 17, turn onto US 17 and drive south for 1.2 miles to
the intersection of US 17 and Harris Neck Road (CR 246), just past the
Smallest Church in America. Turn left onto Harris Neck Road and continue
7.4 miles to the entrance of the refuge.

The background: For more than a quarter of a century, the North
American Butterfly Association has been holding butterfly counts throughout
the United States, Canada, and Mexico. The counts, which are called the
Fourth of July Butterfly Counts, are scheduled on or near July 4.

The counts are designed to provide butterfly experts (lepidopterists) with
valuable information concerning the abundance of the hundreds of species of
butterflies found throughout North America. The surveys are also used to
monitor how weather and the changing face of our landscape are affecting

Butterflies, such as this swallowtail, can often be seen early in the day basking in the sun.

butterflies. The counts are similar to the Christmas Bird Counts in that the goal is to count as many butterflies as possible in a single day in a count circle 15 miles in diameter.

The fun: Butterfly-watching can be fun for the entire family. While being able to identify a host of butterflies is an asset, even those family members that don't know a skipper from a monarch can have fun and play an important role in the count by spotting butterflies that can be identified by others.

Many large butterflies, such as monarchs and tiger swallowtails, can be identified without the use of binoculars. However, trying to identify hairstreaks and other small butterflies with the unaided eye can be a challenge. Consequently, binoculars that permit you to focus on objects as close as 6 feet away can be a real asset. If you use standard binoculars, you will often have to stand so far away from the butterflies you are trying to identify that identification will be difficult.

Butterfly counts provide excellent opportunities for beginning butterfly-watchers to hone their skills. Experienced butterfly-watchers are teamed with those just learning the differences between a pearl crescent and a question mark. A few hours spent with an expert can be more valuable than poring over field guides for hours on end.

Butterflies are often most active when temperatures are warm and skies sunny, so daytime butterfly-watching is most productive. One of the most valuable lessons that can be learned on a butterfly count is where to find butterflies. While butterflies can be found practically anywhere, each species has its own habitat preference. On a count you will learn which wildflowers attract butterflies and also discover such things as why mud puddles and the muddy shorelines of lakes and streams are great places to find butterflies.

As you travel home after the count, your memory will be full of the images of American ladies, sachems, fiery skippers, sleepy oranges, commas, and other fascinating butterflies that flutter about the Georgia countryside.

Food and lodging: A restaurant and an RV park are off I–95, exit 67.

For more information:
U.S. Fish and Wildlife Service
Savannah Coastal Refuges
1000 Business Center Drive
Parkway Business Center, Suite 10
Savannah, GA 31405
(912) 652–4415

North American Butterfly Count
2533 McCart
Fort Worth, TX 76110
(973) 285–0907

Georgia butterflies Web site:
www.geocities.com/mike/chap

20

Summer

A Canyon Treasure

View the spectacular floral show staged by the blooming of the world's largest wild population of the rare plumleaf azalea.

Recommended time: Early July through mid-August. The peak blooming period for the plumleaf azalea in Georgia normally extends from mid-July to the first week in August. The park is open extended hours at this time of year from 7:00 A.M. to 9:00 P.M. daily. Since temperatures and humidity levels are typically high at this time of year, try to enter the canyon early in the day when conditions are most pleasant.

Name and location of site: Providence Canyon State Park, approximately 10 miles from Lumpkin.

Minimum time commitment: Two hours.

What to bring: Camera, towels, spare walking shoes (or waterproof boots or shoes), binoculars, plant and animal field guides, water or other beverage.

Admission fee: Daily parking is $2.00 per vehicle; an annual Georgia ParkPass is $25. Discounts are available for senior citizens.

Directions: In Lumpkin, at the junction of US 27 and Florence Street (SR 39C), turn onto Florence Street and continue west 8 miles to the park entrance.

The background: Providence Canyon State Park's 1,108 acres encompass sixteen canyons. The canyon complex, often called Georgia's Little Grand Canyon, is young in geological time. The erosional process that formed the canyon began in the early part of the nineteenth century when pioneer

Not-So-Plentiful Plumleaf

The azaleas and their close relatives, rhododendrons, are among the showiest woody shrubs found in the Southeast. Most of these flowering woody plants are spring bloomers. However, the rare plumleaf azalea displays its floral show long after the blooms of other native azaleas and rhododendrons have lost their vibrantly colorful blossoms. This large shrub grows upwards of 20 feet tall and blooms from mid- to late summer.

The colors of the plumleaf azalea's flowers range from scarlet to orange. The delicate, open, funnel-shaped, 2-inch blossoms are found in clusters of four to five.

Plumleaf azaleas are becoming increasingly more difficult to find growing in the wild. In the Peach State, the center of the plant's range is along the Chattahoochee River in west-central Georgia. However, nowhere in this state will you find these gorgeous shrubs growing in more abundance than in Providence Canyon. In fact, the canyon is purported to harbor the largest concentration (1,000 plants) of wild plumleaf azaleas in the world.

farmers cleared the land for their crops and livestock. Without its protective vegetation, the area's highly erodible soil quickly began washing away. By the mid 1800s, erosional gullies 3 to 5 feet deep were etched into the countryside. The erosion continues to this day, although it has slowed since reaching the erosion-resistant soils that currently lie at the bottom of the canyon some 150 feet below the canyon rim.

The fun: To reach the plumleaf azaleas, you must descend into Providence Canyon. Before beginning your adventure, pick up a map of the canyon at the visitors center to ensure that you don't get lost.

Your trek begins at the trailhead immediately behind the visitors center. A wide and well-maintained trail winds its way through a series of switchbacks that ease your steep descent into the canyon. At this time of year, the thick foliage of the oaks, hickories, dogwoods, and pines growing on the side of the

The largest wild population of plumleaf azaleas in the world grows in Providence Canyon.

canyon shades visitors from the hot summer sun. As you approach the canyon floor, a few plumleaf azaleas can be seen growing alongside the trail. They appear as splashes of red in the subdued light of the forest.

Once you reach the bottom of the canyon, the trail seemingly ends at the edge of an extremely shallow, slow-moving stream. To enjoy the full flavor of the azaleas' brilliant midsummer floral display, walk along the streambed. Walking is wet but relatively easy. The water is only inches deep and flows over a bed of hard, sandy clay. Some of the largest concentrations of plumleaf azaleas are found in the canyons to your left (north). Most of the tall azaleas are found growing at the very edge of the water, providing a multitude of viewing and photographing opportunities. Butterflies flit among the scarlet floral trumpets that festoon the shrubs hugging the stream. In the distance, the exposed earth of the canyon walls is tinted in subtle pastel shades of salmon, white, orange, purple, and pink. Summer insects and birds provide the only sounds heard. Finding a more relaxing setting would be difficult.

While there are many beautiful and fascinating plants found in the canyon, one of most intriguing is the bigleaf magnolia. Its extremely large leaves—up to 12 inches wide and 30 inches long—easily identify this tree. Although its large flowers (10 to 18 inches in diameter) cannot be seen at this time of year, you can see its massive, round, red hairy fruits that look much like rose-colored softballs.

For those that want to hike, 3 miles of hiking trails wind through and around the canyon. In addition, overnight camping is permitted along a 7-mile backpacking trail.

Visitors can learn about the fascinating history of the canyon at the visitors center (open from 8:00 A.M. to 5:00 P.M. daily). The spectacular views of the canyon can be enjoyed from any one of sixteen overlooks scattered along the canyon rim.

Food and lodging: Two restaurants and a couple of delicatessens are 8 miles from the park in Lumpkin. Pioneer camping (available only to groups; facilities consist of tent sites and primitive privies) is available in the park. Ten cottages and forty-four tent, trailer, and RV sites are available 8 miles away at Florence Marina State Park. The closest motel is in Richland, 16 miles from the canyon.

For more information:

Georgia Department of Natural Resources
Parks and Historic Sites Division
205 Butler Street SE, Suite 1352
Atlanta, GA 30334
(404) 656–3530 or (770) 389–7275 (when calling from metro Atlanta)
or
Providence Canyon State Park
Route 1, Box 158
Lumpkin, GA 31815
(229) 838–6202

21

Sea Turtles by Starlight

Loggerhead sea turtles nest on this beach, giving visitors an opportunity to turtle-track and find one of these endangered reptiles.

Recommended time: June through mid-August.

Name and location of site: Jekyll Island, 82 miles (one hour and twenty-five minutes) south of Savannah.

Minimum time commitment: One and a half to two hours.

What to bring: Insect repellent.

Admission fee: The daily entry fee is $3.00 per vehicle. A daily $4.00-per-vehicle permit allows one reentry to the island. Both three-day ($12) and seven-day ($24) vehicle passes are available. Both of these permits provide unlimited reentry privileges. Participation fees for the turtle walk are $5.00 for adults and $3.00 for students.

Directions: From the junction of I–95 (exit 29) and US 17 just south of Brunswick, turn left (east) onto US 17 and continue to the junction of Jekyll Island Road. Turn right on Jekyll Island Road and drive to the junction of Riverview Drive (6.4 miles). Turn left on Riverview Drive and continue 0.5 mile to the junction of Old Village Boulevard. Drive 0.3 mile to the intersection of Stable Road. You will see the Museum Visitors Center on the right.

The background: The loggerhead sea turtle is the only sea turtle that regularly nests along the Georgia coast. The nesting season begins in early May and ends by mid-August. During this time, nesting female loggerheads come ashore an average of four times to lay eggs. The eggs are laid in nests

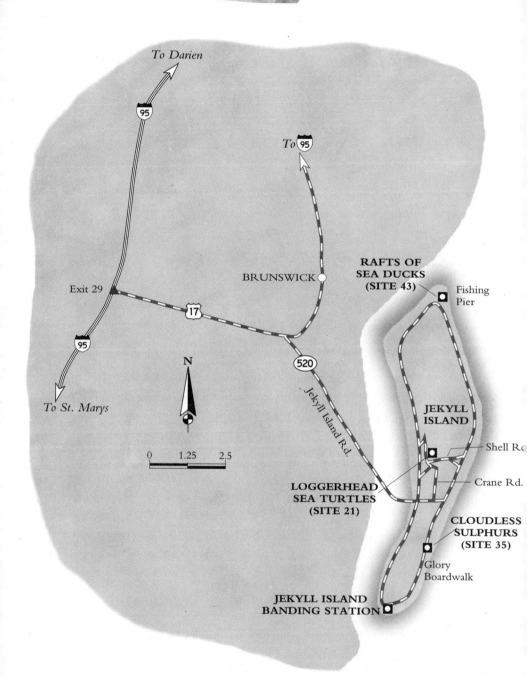

To Darien

95

To 95

Exit 29

17

95

To St. Marys

N

0   1.25   2.5

BRUNSWICK

520

Jekyll Island Rd.

RAFTS OF
SEA DUCKS
(SITE 43)

Fishing
Pier

JEKYLL
ISLAND

Shell Ro

Crane Rd.

LOGGERHEAD
SEA TURTLES
(SITE 21)

CLOUDLESS
SULPHURS
(SITE 35)

Glory
Boardwalk

JEKYLL ISLAND
BANDING STATION

dug in the sand above the high water mark. Fifty to 170 eggs are laid in each nest. If the nesting effort is successful, the hatchlings will emerge from the sand sixty days after the eggs are laid. Experts believe that a female loggerhead must be between twenty and thirty years old before laying her first clutch of eggs. Females usually nest only once every two to three years.

These nesting attempts are closely monitored on Georgia's beaches. The Georgia Wildlife Resources Division's Nongame Wildlife/Natural Heritage Section, working with the U.S. Fish and Wildlife Service, National Park Service, private foundations, and volunteers, conduct daily nest patrols throughout the nesting season. Since nest predation can run as high as 100 percent on some islands, nests are protected from predators such as raccoons with metal screening. After hatching, each nest is dug up and hatching success determined.

The fun: One of the best ways to learn about loggerhead sea turtle nesting and conservation is to take one of the nightly turtle walks conducted by trained guides. During these walks, visitors are taken on 2-mile treks along the beach in quest of nesting sea turtles.

Your adventure begins at the Museum Visitors Center. Plan on showing up around 9:00 P.M. Before leaving for the beach, you are shown a short video on sea turtle nesting, which is followed by a brief question-and-answer session. Afterward everyone loads up in their cars and heads for the beach.

For the next hour and a half, you will slowly walk approximately 2 miles of beach looking for nesting sea turtles. During this time it is extremely important that you carefully follow the directions given to you by your guide. The last thing that you want to do is be responsible for causing a turtle to abandon her nesting attempt.

One of the best ways to spot a nesting turtle is to find the tracks made by the turtle as she emerges from the water. As you might expect, the tracks left by an animal as large as a loggerhead sea turtle are quite impressive. At times females will crawl out of the ocean and then return without ever laying an egg. These "false" crawls can sometimes be caused when people disrupt the turtle after she comes ashore.

If you are lucky, you will find a crawl made by a turtle that is actively nesting. If so, you may have the rare opportunity to watch as the female methodically digs her nest using her flippers. After the egg chamber has been constructed, she will begin laying her clutch of eggs. Once the eggs have been laid, she will cover the eggs and try to hide her nest. She then begins her laborious trek back to the sea.

Loggerheads on the Brink

The loggerhead sea turtle is a large marine turtle that tips the scales at between 165 and 330 pounds and measures 31 to 43 inches long. Typically, loggerheads are brown to reddish brown in color. The loggerhead sea turtle gets its name from the fact that its head is disproportionately larger than its body.

Like the other sea turtles that are found in Georgia waters, the loggerhead sea turtle's name appears on the Federal Endangered Species List. We humans are primarily responsible for the population declines suffered by the loggerhead. They are still harvested for food, as are their eggs, and they are losing valuable nesting habitats in many parts of their range due to alteration of beaches for erosion control. One of the greatest human-related threats to loggerheads is commercial fishing. Loggerhead and other sea turtles are often accidentally captured in shrimp nets. To alleviate this problem, the shrimping industry and federal and state conservation agencies are working together. Since 1989 the use of turtle excluder devices (TEDs), which allow turtles captured in shrimp nets to escape before they drown, have greatly reduced this loss. Prior to the use of TEDs, commercial shrimp nets killed 5,000 to 50,000 loggerhead sea turtles in the waters off the southeastern United States. Another significant cause of mortality is boat strikes. In Georgia waters, 15 percent of all loggerhead deaths can be attributed to boats.

Upwards of 1,375 loggerhead sea turtle nests are found annually along Georgia beaches. The fact that this has not changed significantly in more than a decade is a good indication that much work needs to be done before we can safely say we have pulled the loggerhead sea turtle back from the brink of extinction.

Loggerhead sea turtle hatchlings dash to the sea.

Here are some things to keep in mind if you should encounter a nesting sea turtle while walking the beach on your own:

- Never shine a flashlight in the face of a turtle.
- Don't take flash pictures of a sea turtle.
- Don't attempt to get close to a turtle until she begins laying her eggs.
- Don't try to touch the turtle or its eggs.

If you take a turtle walk from mid-July to mid-August, you might happen across hatchlings making their way to the sea. Young loggerhead sea turtles usually emerge at night, look for the light of the horizon, and then run toward the sea. At this critical time lights along the beach can disorient them, and lights from a building or highway can cause the hatchlings to scamper away from the ocean. When this happens, they have little chance of survival. Even under the best conditions, the odds are weighed heavily against them. Only one out of every 10,000 hatchlings lives to adulthood.

Food and lodging: There are many restaurants and motels on Jekyll Island.

For more information:

Turtle Walks: The Sea Turtle Project
196 Stable Road
Jekyll Island, GA 31527
(912) 635–2284

22

Summer

A View from the Top of Georgia

See the equivalent of 1,000 miles of varied habitat in only a 0.5-mile climb up Brasstown Bald, Georgia's highest point.

Recommended time: July or August.

Name and location of site: Brasstown Bald (Chattahoochee National Forest), approximately 20 miles from Helen.

Minimum time commitment: Two hours.

What to bring: Camera, binoculars.

Admission fee: $2.00 parking fee.

Directions: From Helen travel north on SR 75 for 12 miles to the junction of SR 75 and SR 180. Turn left (west) on SR 180 and continue 5 miles to the junction of SR 180 and SR 180 Spur. Turn left onto SR 180 Spur and drive 2.9 miles to the top of the mountain.

The background: Brasstown Bald is the highest mountain in Georgia, standing 4,784 feet above sea level. It is found within the Chattahoochee National Forest. Brasstown Bald is truly unique. Besides being the state's highest point, it marks the southern range limit for many plants and animals.

According to Cherokee legend, "balds," mountains topped with bare rock, were created by their Great Spirit. Supposedly, balds were formed at a time when a terrible flying beast would swoop down and attempt to snatch and devour helpless Native American children. Tired of the terror caused by the flying monster, the Cherokees cleared away the forest growing on top of many mountains in an attempt to capture the beast. When the Cherokees

A view from Brasstown Bald, the highest point in Georgia.

prayed to the Great Spirit to help them, he slew the terrible creature, returned the children, and kept the mountaintops bare to this day.

Another Cherokee legend tells of a great flood that engulfed the earth. The only people that survived the catastrophe were those riding in a giant canoe. These fortunate few beached their canoe atop Brasstown Bald. The mountaintop was cleared by the Great Spirit, and the Native Americans grew crops to feed themselves until the floodwaters receded.

The Cherokee name for Brasstown Bald is Enotah. It is believed that the name Brasstown arose from early settlers confusing the Cherokee word *itse-yi,* meaning "place of fresh green," with *untsaiyi,* the Cherokee word for brass.

Georgia's only cloud forest is found here. The northern slope of this majestic mountain is regularly bathed in moisture from clouds, creating a haven for wildflowers, trees, and lichens.

In an effort to protect the unique natural areas around Brasstown Bald, in 1986 Congress designated the 11,405 acres immediately adjacent to the bald as a Wilderness Area.

The fun: Your adventure begins as you slowly ascend the long snakelike road leading to the lofty mountain pinnacle. The road winds its way through a seemingly endless expanse of forest. From time to time you will catch a glimpse of the visitors center that sits atop the bald. The road finally ends at the large parking lot short of the peak.

To reach the summit, you can ride a shuttle or hike a 0.5-mile paved trail. The trail is very steep, climbing 500 feet. If you decide to take the trail, your short trek is botanically the equivalent to making a thousand-mile journey northward. As you continue upward, note that the trailside trees get shorter. Eventually the trail passes through an oak forest. While these red and white oaks are decades old, they haven't aged well. Trying to grow in the mountain's harsh environmental conditions has left them stubby and twisted. At the very top, dwarf willows similar to those that grow in the tundra can be found.

At the peak, visitors enjoy temperatures that are significantly lower than those at the bottom of the mountain. Temperatures on Brasstown Bald average ten degrees cooler than those in the lowlands. The highest and lowest temperatures ever recorded on the mountain are 84 degrees Fahrenheit and 27 degrees Fahrenheit below zero, respectively.

At the visitors center, stairs and elevators take you to the observation decks, where there are breathtaking views of the surrounding landscape. In fact, on a clear day, it is possible to see four states and Atlanta. It is also exciting to watch a storm moving over the landscape.

The displays housed in the visitors center are among the best in Georgia. These exhibits graphically depict the colorful natural, geologic, and human history of the Brasstown Bald and the surrounding southern Appalachians. Displays range from artifacts made by Native Americans to dioramas featuring native animals and plants. There are even animated full-size figures that tell about the U.S. Forest Service's efforts to protect and manage the natural resources in the Chattahoochee National Forest. Videos are screened in The Mountaintop Theater throughout the day.

No trip to Brasstown Bald would be complete without a picnic. Picnic tables are located at the south end of the parking lot. While eating, keep an eye out for common ravens. These black birds have massive bills and are a full 6 inches larger than the American crow. Their call is unlike the familiar *caaw* of the American crow and is best described as a low-pitched *gronk*. North Georgia is the southern limit of the common raven's range, and Brasstown Bald is one of the few places where it can be seen with any regularity.

Food and lodging: Four lodgings and no restaurants are located with 15 miles of the area.

For more information:
Blairsville Ranger Office
U.S. Forest Service
1881 Highway 515
Blairsville, GA 30512
(706) 745–6928
or
Brasstown Bald Visitor Information Center
(706) 896–2556

23

Summer

Gopher Tortoises Dig the Heat

The threatened Georgia State Reptile finds its preferred habitat in General Coffee State Park's rare longleaf pine–wiregrass community.

Recommended time: May through August.

Name and location of site: General Coffee State Park, 6 miles outside of Douglas.

Minimum time commitment: Two hours.

What to bring: Binoculars, camera.

Admission fee: Daily parking is $2.00 per vehicle; an annual Georgia ParkPass is $25. Discounts are available for senior citizens.

Directions: In Douglas, take SR 32 east for 6 miles to the park entrance on the left.

The background: The gopher tortoise is the Georgia State Reptile. This large (up to 15 inches in length) land turtle inhabits one of the most endangered ecosystems in North America—the longleaf pine–wiregrass community. Today less than 3 percent of the longleaf pine forest exists. With the widespread destruction of its preferred habitat, gopher tortoise populations have plummeted. In response to this drastic decline, the gopher tortoise is listed as threatened on the Georgia Protected Species List.

The fun: General Coffee State Park is an ideal place to watch gopher tortoises. While they can regularly be seen along any of the park's roads, they are most often spotted along those that traverse the western end of the park. The best way to find these turtles is to drive or walk along the park's roadways. If

An adult gopher tortoise searches for food.

you don't see them on your first pass, turn around and try again. When you come across a gopher tortoise, don't try to pick it up. Instead, observe it from a distance. If you don't approach too closely, the tortoise will continue its normal routine.

Gopher tortoises are quite active on warm days. While you can find them throughout the year, they seem to be most active from May through August. The best viewing times fall between 10:00 A.M. and 2:00 P.M. During this, the hottest time of the day, these slow-moving animals meander about looking for food. The remainder of the day is spent in the safety of their burrows.

Observing gopher tortoise behavior is always fascinating. Gopher tortoises will often bob their heads when they encounter another tortoise. At times they will bob their heads and then ram one another in an attempt to flip each other over. In spring, the mating time of the gopher tortoise, you might even see one or more males chasing a female.

If, for some reason, you don't find a gopher tortoise, you will see their burrows, whose entrances are wider than they are tall. A distinct mound or apron of sand, where female gopher tortoises typically lay their eggs, is found at the

Not Just a "Hoover Chicken"

The gopher tortoise ranges from southeastern Louisiana eastward through southern Mississippi, Alabama, Georgia, and Florida to the southern tip of South Carolina and is usually found in areas characterized by deep sandy soils, open tree canopies, abundant grasses, and other herbaceous plants. This habitat is maintained with periodic fires.

The mainstays of this tortoise's diet are grasses, such as wiregrass; legumes; and other low-growing plants. Gopher tortoises will also dine on gopher apples and various fruits and berries.

Gopher tortoises spend much of their time living in burrows that they excavate. These burrows can measure more than 47 feet long but average only 15 feet long. The burrow ends in a chamber that is large enough for the turtle to turn around in. Gopher tortoises often dig more than one burrow, using them to escape the periodic fires that sweep across this landscape and as shelter from the heat of summer and cold of winter.

Gopher tortoise burrows are also valuable sanctuaries for a host of other animals. Some of the animals that are either temporary or permanent burrow residents include quail, otters, coyotes, red foxes, eastern diamondback rattlesnakes, indigo snakes, toads, opossums, and more than thirty-eight species of invertebrates (animals without backbones), such as insects, ticks and spiders.

Gopher tortoises live longer than most animals, and it is thought that they may live to be eighty years old or more. Finding gopher tortoises that are twenty-five years old or older is common.

Interestingly, female gopher tortoises don't reach maturity until they are ten to twenty-one years old. In comparison, males mature when they reach the age of sixteen to eighteen. The fact that gopher tortoises take so long to mature, coupled with the fact that in Georgia a female gopher tortoise's nesting efforts produce fewer than six hatchlings every ten years, hinders this species' ability to reverse its downward population trend.

Indeed, gopher tortoises face an uncertain future. Their habitat is being destroyed at an alarming rate, they reproduce very slowly, they are often killed on our highways, and they are sometimes collected as pets. Although they were eaten by some humans in the past (during the Depression they were called "Hoover chickens"), they are now protected by state law. Finding ways to conserve our precious gopher tortoise populations will be one of the challenges that face conservationists in the twenty-first century.

entrance of the burrow. If you find the entrance to a gopher tortoise hole covered with cobwebs, a tortoise probably isn't using it. Occupied burrows are spiderweb-free, and the soil around the entrance will show signs of animal use.

After watching the gopher tortoise roam through its habitat, one has to be impressed with the animal's ability to survive in this harsh, dry, sandy landscape. While it may not be to our liking, it suits the gopher tortoise just fine.

Food and lodging: At least three motels and five restaurants are located within 10 miles of the park. In addition, the Burnham house (a restored nineteenth-century cabin) and twenty-five campsites are available in the park.

For more information:
General Coffee State Park
46 John Coffee Road
Nicholls, GA 31554
(912) 384–7082

24

Summer

Urban Shorebirds

This water treatment facility within the state's largest metropolitan area provides a critical feeding habitat for migratory shorebirds and waterfowl.

Recommended time: Late July through September.

Name and location of site: E. L. Huie Water Treatment Facility, 19 miles (thirty minutes) south of Atlanta.

Minimum time commitment: One to two hours.

What to bring: Binoculars, spotting scope, camera, field guide to birds.

Admission fee: None.

Directions: From Atlanta: From the junction of I–20 and I–75 drive south on I–75 to US 41 (exit 235). Turn right onto Tara Boulevard. Continue down Tara Boulevard 6.5 miles and turn left onto Freeman Road. Head south on Freeman Road for 0.25 mile to the junction of Freeman Road and Dixon Industrial Boulevard. Turn left on Dixon Industrial Boulevard and continue 0.2 mile to the entrance of the water-treatment ponds on the left. The entrance road veers off to the left and continues up the embankment to the ponds.

The background: Remarkably, this water treatment facility, located in the state's largest metropolitan area, is one of the best places in Georgia to view migratory shorebirds and waterfowl. Here, practically in the shadows of Atlanta's skyline, shorebirds winging their way to and from their breeding grounds and wintering areas stop to rest and feed. Stopover areas such as this

Migrating shorebirds flock to the muddy banks of the impoundments at the E.L. Huie Water Treatment Facility.

are critical to the survival of this fascinating and diverse group of birds.

The bottoms of these man-made ponds are alive with invertebrates, which are an abundant source of food for the birds. However, this bounty of food is only available when water levels in the impoundments are low enough for the birds to probe the wet soils that form the bottoms of the ponds. Since these ponds are periodically flooded and drained as part of the facility's water treatment activities, you never know which ponds will have the exposed mudflats preferred by the feeding birds.

The Clayton County Water Authority has long recognized that it can conduct normal operations and still provide wildlife-viewing opportunities for the public. As a result, the facility stands as an outstanding example of multiple use.

The fun: Most people have the notion that the fall bird migration doesn't begin until the leaves begin to turn in October. In reality, many birds begin their annual trek southward in midsummer. Consequently, a host of birds, particularly shorebirds, that begin to arrive in Georgia in midsummer have already passed through the Peach State by the time folks begin looking for them.

A Place to Rest and Refuel

Shorebirds are among the most traveled birds found anywhere in the world. Many shorebirds nest in the tundra and spend part of their lives along ocean beaches, mudflats, and the shorelines of inland lakes. The semipalmated plover, for example, breeds in Alaska and northern Canada and winters as far south as the southern half of South America.

Aside from those shorebirds that either breed or winter in Georgia, the only times we see them are during their biannual migrations to and from their breeding and nesting grounds. During these brief interludes, the birds stop at places where they can rest and refuel before resuming their journeys. Good stopover areas are used by generations of migratory shorebirds. The problem is that as our human population continues to expand, these stopover areas are being converted to homesites, roads, malls, and agricultural fields. When this happens the birds must fly farther to find resting and feeding sites or face crowding on what wetlands remain. The loss of these critical habitats threatens the survival of many of these birds.

The E. L. Huie Water Treatment Facility provides wildlife-watchers with an ideal opportunity to see these early migrants. As with most wildlife, the best times to view these long-distance migrants are early and late in the day. One of the added advantages of going then is that temperatures are more moderate. However, good viewing opportunities can be enjoyed any time of day.

When you arrive at the facility, slowly drive the roads that ring the holding ponds. You will find that the shorebirds will congregate in those ponds that have exposed mudflats. Once you have found feeding shorebirds, get out of your car and set up your spotting scope.

While some shorebirds will allow you to approach within binocular range, they are best viewed with a spotting scope. Since the area is a popular wildlife-viewing site, often you will find other parties watching the birds. They will often be happy to let you view the birds through their scopes and even help you with identification.

Over the course of a migration, more than a dozen species of shorebirds can be seen here. This list includes both greater and lesser yellowlegs, semipalmated plovers, killdeer, common snipes, dowitchers, dunlins, pectoral sandpipers, western sandpipers, semipalmated sandpipers, spotted sandpipers, solitary sandpipers, as well as rarities such as buff-bellied and Baird's sandpipers.

Your wildlife-watching experience can be made more enjoyable by carefully watching the behavior of each species of bird you encounter. A bird's behavior can help you identify it and to also understand more about its lifestyle.

One of the most fascinating things to watch is how the length of each bird's bill and legs dictates where it will feed. Many of these shorebirds feed by probing the mud for invertebrates, and many different species can feed along the same mud bank without actually competing with one another for food. For example, the smallest shorebird you will find at the facility is the least sandpiper. This mite (5 to 6 inches long) travels in small flocks and feeds along the edge of the water. In contrast, the much larger dowitcher (9.5 to 12 inches long) can wade out into deeper water and probe the mud with a characteristic sewing machine–like motion.

The greater yellowlegs, on the other hand, has a totally different method of feeding. This tall wader dashes about, skimming small animals from the top of the water with its long slender bill.

The spotted sandpiper is a good example of a bird whose behavior is an aid to identification. This shorebird is usually seen alone. It will be found walking along the shorelines of the ponds, bobbing its tail as it goes.

While shorebirds are often the main attraction at this time of year, the holding ponds are also havens for other water and wading birds. Look for belted kingfishers sitting atop light poles and watching for unwary fish. Double-crested cormorants can often be seen drying their wings as green herons, great blue herons, great egrets, and other wading birds hunt the shorelines. Canada geese and mallards can be spotted on most visits. The first migratory waterfowl, the blue-winged teal, makes its first appearance in midsummer. Over the next few weeks it is followed by the green-winged teal, pintail, shoveler, lesser scaup, ring-necked duck, American wigeon, gadwall, and other ducks.

When you are standing on the dike of an impoundment at the E. L. Huie Water Treatment Facility and enjoying the view of hundreds of shore, water, and wading birds, if it were not for the sounds of traffic and the sight of concrete and steel structures scattered along the shoreline, it would be easy to believe that you are visiting some secluded wetland miles from the city.

Food and lodging: A wide variety of restaurants and lodging is available within 15 miles of the destination.

For more information:
The Wetland Center of the Clayton County Water Authority
2755 Freeman Road
Hampton, GA 30228
(470) 603–5606

25

Summer

A Trek into a Mountain

This natural cave is one of the few in Georgia open for public viewing and partial exploration.

Recommended time: July through August.

Name and location of site: Rolater Park, near the town of Cave Spring.

Minimum time commitment: One hour.

What to bring: Flashlight, slip-resistant shoes. If you choose to swim in the pool, you'll need a bathing suit and a towel.

Admission fee: $1.00 per person to visit the cave.

Directions: From the traffic light in Cave Spring, continue straight on Old Cedar Town Road 0.2 mile to the entrance to Rolater Park, which is just beyond the bridge spanning Cedar Creek. Turn left into the park and follow the signs to the entrance of the cave at the back right corner of the park.

The background: Most people consider caves to be dark, foreboding places. While they are dark, they're also very fragile habitats that are home to a host of unique and fascinating animals, many of which live out their lives without ever seeing the light of day. Most of Georgia's caves cannot be visited safely by those who are not highly trained and equipped with specialized caving equipment. This is not the case with the cave located along the back side of the twenty-nine-acre Rolater Park in Cave Spring. A small portion of this cave is open to the public and provides a great opportunity to become acquainted with this unique natural habitat.

Watch your head as you explore these mountain passageways.

Visitors should avoid disturbing the habitat when they enter a cave. When you leave, no trace of your visit should be left behind. Some previous visitors have damaged the cave by leaving behind graffiti and trash and disturbing cave formations. Sadly, some damage done by these thoughtless individuals may never heal.

Approximately four million gallons of crystal-clear water flow from a mineral spring found deep within the dark recesses of this natural-erosion cave. The water is advertised as being the "purest water in the state," and it is also purported to have medicinal qualities.

Water flowing from the cave feeds into a unique one-and-a-half-acre swimming pool, which is shaped like the state of Georgia. It is the second largest swimming pool in the Peach State.

The fun: Begin your outing by visiting the cave. Before entering, make sure that your flashlight is working. While the cave is lit, a flashlight will come in handy when exploring those sections of the cave that are dimly lit. As you enter the cave, you are greeted with a blast of cool air. The cave's natural air-conditioning system cools the cave's air to a chilly 56 degrees Fahrenheit year-round.

Approximately 25 yards from the cave's entrance, the cave narrows to a gateway (about 4 square feet) leading to a large open room. Take your time and scan the rock walls; they are festooned with many stalactites and stalagmites in varying stages of formation.

Off to the left of the main room, a side tunnel leads to a smaller chamber. To enter this area, you have to pass through a passageway that is only about 3 feet tall. Both the passageway and the room beyond are poorly illuminated, so it is a good idea to use your flashlight to make sure you don't bump your head as you make your way through the narrow opening. Upon entering the room you will find a small pool on the right.

Returning to the main room, you can see another passageway to the right. This tunnel leads upward to a dead end. If you decide to explore this area, watch your step; the path is quite steep, shrouded in shadows, and wet.

After your visit to the cave, there is plenty to see and do in Rolater Park. Stop by the large, shallow pool located near the cave entrance. It is stocked with large trout, which can be coaxed into a feeding frenzy when given food that can be purchased at the cave entrance. Also on park grounds, you can visit historic nineteenth-century buildings, enjoy a picnic lunch, or go for a dip in the park's novel swimming pool.

Food and lodging: Four restaurants, a bed-and-breakfast, a motel, and an RV park are situated in and around the city of Cave Spring.

For more information:
Mrs. Emily Highnote
Cave Springs, GA 30124
(706) 777–3961, (706) 777–3962, or (706) 777–8439

26

Summer

A Night Under the Stars

Whether or not you know the difference between a crab nebula and a crab cake, you will enjoy an evening under the stars at the Hard Labor Creek Observatory.

Recommended time: July through August.

Name and location of site: Georgia State University's Hard Labor Creek Observatory in Hard Labor Creek State Park, 45 miles (fifty-five minutes) east of Atlanta.

Minimum time commitment: Two hours.

What to bring: No special equipment is needed to enjoy this event.

Admission fee: Free. If you visit surrounding Hard Labor Creek State Park, a daily parking fee of $2.00 per vehicle or an annual Georgia ParkPass ($25) is required. Discounts are available for senior citizens. No additional fee is charged for the astronomy programs.

Directions: From Rutledge take Fairplay Road 2 miles to Hard Labor Creek State Park. Stay on Fairplay Road past the golf course and across a bridge with a lake on your left. After you have passed over the bridge, the road proceeds up a hill. Just past the crest of the hill, a dirt road will intersect from the right. Turn right on this road and drive up to the observatory.

The background: The Hard Labor Creek Observatory is in the 5,804-acre Hard Labor Creek State Park. The state park is a short drive away from Georgia State University, which operates the observatory. The park is far enough from the city to experience dark skies, not affected by the artificial lights that make the use of optical telescopes difficult if not impossible.

One Saturday night a month from March through October, the observatory staff holds an open house for anyone interested in astronomy. These events are held from sunset until 11:00 P.M. or midnight. When it is raining or the skies are cloudy, the astronomers present fascinating astronomy programs. The research facility houses one 40-inch telescope, two 16-inch telescopes, and numerous 12.5-inch telescopes. One of the 16-inch telescopes and the 12.5-inch telescopes are used during open houses.

The fun: It is difficult not to be captivated with the universe. Unmanned space probes that have delved into the far reaches of our solar system, coupled with the startling findings of astronomers throughout the world, have given us a wealth of mind-boggling information about the universe. With each startling discovery, interest in astronomy grows. However, since high-quality telescopes are extremely expensive, most people who long to gaze at distant planets and other heavenly bodies never get the opportunity to do so. Attending an open house at the Hard Labor Creek Observatory will change this.

On these special nights, 12.5-inch telescopes are set up outside the observatory for public use. In addition, visitors are invited inside the observatory to view objects in space through the giant 16-inch telescope. One thing that makes these open houses so special is the fact that expert astronomers are leading you every step of the way as you take a visual journey through the universe.

A word of caution: Should you arrive at the observatory after dark, please turn off your lights as you drive up to the facility. The flash of your headlights can blind those using telescopes.

Food and lodging: Twenty cottages and fifty-one tent, trailer, and RV sites are in the park, and fifteen restaurants and nine motels are within 15 miles of the park.

For more information:

Hard Labor Creek State Park
P.O. Box 147
Rutledge, GA 30663
(706) 557–3001

27

Summer

Hummingbird Hangout

The aerial acrobatics of squadrons of rare ruby-throated humming-birds are a delight to watch while visiting this demonstration area.

Recommended time: End of July through early September.

Name and location of site: Nongame-Endangered Wildlife Program Office Backyard Wildlife Habitat Demonstration Area, 56 miles (one hour) south of Atlanta.

Minimum time commitment: One hour.

What to bring: Binoculars, camera.

Admission fee: None.

Directions: From Atlanta: From the junction of US 19 and I–75 (exit 235) in south Atlanta, travel south 49 miles on I–75 to SR 18 (exit 185) at Forsyth. Turn left (east) on SR 18 and drive 7 miles to the entrance sign for the Rum Creek Wildlife Management Area and Nongame-Endangered Wildlife Program Office. Turn left on the gravel road just beyond the sign. Pass through two gates; the office and demonstration area are on the left side of the road just beyond the second gate.

The background: The ruby-throated hummingbird is the only hummingbird known to nest east of the Mississippi River. In Georgia, ruby-throated hummingbirds nest throughout the entire state.

The state office of the Georgia Nongame-Endangered Wildlife Program is situated on the Rum Creek Wildlife Management Area. This is not your typical office setting. The grounds surrounding this rural office are used to

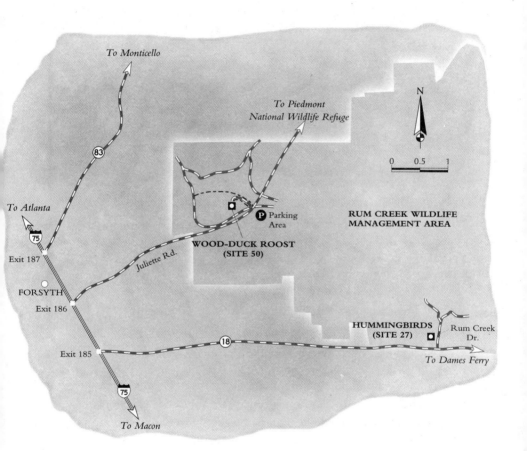

To Monticello

To Piedmont
National Wildlife Refuge

N

0   0.5   1

83

To Atlanta

75

Exit 187

RUM CREEK WILDLIFE
MANAGEMENT AREA

Parking
Area

WOOD-DUCK ROOST
(SITE 50)

Juliette Rd.

FORSYTH

Exit 186

HUMMINGBIRDS
(SITE 27)

Rum Creek
Dr.

Exit 185

18

To Dames Ferry

75

To Macon

During the summer, a steady stream of hummingbirds visit the feeders at the office of the Nongame-Endangered Wildlife Program.

demonstrate plantings and other management practices that homeowners can use to transform their yards into havens for wildlife.

Ruby-throated hummingbirds begin to arrive in Georgia in early March. From then until October, their aerial acrobatics provide countless hours of entertainment for homeowners that attract these tiny birds to their backyards with feeders and food plants.

The number of hummingbirds visiting backyards in Georgia begins to swell in July. There are three primary reasons for this sudden increase: First, young hummingbirds raised during local breeders' first nesting attempts have fledged and are feeding on their own. Second, the first of the northern migrants are already heading south, using backyards throughout the state as refueling stations. Third, our local hummingbirds are beginning to put on weight in preparation for making their southbound migration.

These numbers eventually peak in late August and September, when fifty to one hundred or more hummingbirds may use a backyard on any given day. At this time, hummingbird-watching is at its best. Sadly though, since most homeowners or public facilities don't attract large concentrations of hummingbirds, few get to see this wildlife spectacle.

The fun: The best way to view the hummingbirds at the demonstration area is to sit quietly in the chairs provided on the front porch of the Nongame-Endangered Wildlife Program Office. Here you will have a panoramic view of most of the hummingbird plants growing in the yard, as well as a battery of feeders hung beneath the porch overhang. Typically the hummingbirds will divide their feeding forays between the feeders and the plants blooming in the yard. Don't be surprised if you don't see many hummingbirds when you first arrive. However, once you have settled in the birds should show up.

Early in the summer hummingbirds regularly feed throughout the day. By September, though, hummingbird migration is in full swing. As a result, you will see more hummers if you visit this site early or late in the day since hummingbird migration seems heaviest during the middle of the day.

One of the first questions that pops into most people's minds when they see lots of hummingbirds is, "How many birds am I looking at?" Banding studies have determined that the best way to estimate hummingbird numbers at this time of year is to count the largest number of birds you see at any one time and multiply that number by six. In other words, if twenty is the greatest number of hummingbirds that you can count, the yard is probably being used by 120 hummers.

You will notice that as the birds feed all around you they don't all look the same. Only the adult male ruby-throated hummingbird has the classic ruby-red gorget. Young males will have thin black streaks extending down their throats. Some will even sport one or two ruby-colored gorget feathers, which will be in the center of their throats and look much like small tie tacks. Older juvenile males might even have as many as five or six gorget feathers. It is next to impossible to sift out young-of-the-year females from adult females.

When the birds are perched on feeders, look carefully at their legs; you might see a tiny, shiny metal band affixed to one leg. If you do, you will know that this bird has been banded. Each year hundreds of hummingbirds are banded at this location since they are being studied as part of a long-term hummingbird migration study. If you are lucky, you even get to witness hummingbirds being banded during your visit to the demonstration area. Typically, banding is conducted during the morning or late afternoon. Since the banders don't operate on a set schedule, if you are interested in watching hummingbird banders at work, call ahead to see if banding will be going on during your visit.

Before you leave, take a walk around the yard and see what plants have been planted for hummingbirds. You might find some plants that might help turn your backyard into a haven for hummingbirds.

Food and lodging: Within 10 miles of the site are one campground, eleven motels, and more than two dozen restaurants.

For more information:

Georgia Wildlife Resources Division
Nongame-Endangered Wildlife Program
116 Rum Creek Drive
Forsyth, GA 31029
(478) 994–1438

28

Searching for Sea Lilies Hundreds of Miles from the Ocean

Fossil remains of sea lilies that lived on the ocean floor millions of years ago appear alongside roadbeds in this national forest.

Recommended time: September.

Name and location of site: Chattahoochee National Forest, 41 miles (forty-five minutes) northwest of Cartersville.

Minimum time commitment: One hour.

What to bring: Trowel.

Admission fee: None.

Directions: From Gore take US 27 for 0.75 mile to FR 254. Take a right and park on the side of the road.

The background: Crinoids are marine animals that look so much like modern-day plants that they are often called sea lilies. Their heads resembled flowers, and these "blooms" were made up of five or multiples of five arms. These arms captured minute sea life called plankton. The flowers were borne on "stems" attached to the ocean floor. Some crinoids had stems that were only inches long; however, the stems of others reached 70 feet or more in length. Washerlike plates supported the stems, and it took literally thousands of these disks to support one of these strange creatures.

The crinoids found at this site lived 310 to 345 million years ago. In fact, sea lilies lived millions of years before the dinosaurs. These ancient plants flourished in the clear, shallow waters of ancient seas. In fact, they were so

The remains of a sea lily that lived millions of years ago.

numerous in some places that their calcium-rich disks formed deposits of limestone.

Along this narrow roadbed you are most likely to find sections of crinoid stems. They will appear much like Life Savers and measure less than 0.5 inch in diameter and have single holes in their centers. Native Americans were known to use these odd objects in necklaces.

Millions of years ago, crinoids were one of the most common animals found in the ocean. Today, the creatures whose remains are found along this rural road are extinct. However, about 650 species of crinoids, which are related to starfish and sea urchins, still live in our oceans. Humans rarely see these creatures, though, as they live in water that is 1,000 feet or more deep. In addition, unlike most of the ancient sea lilies, modern crinoids are free-swimming.

The fun: Fossil-hunting is a real treasure hunt: You never know what you will find. It is something that oldsters and youngsters can do. Instead of searching for gems or precious metals, you are seeking the fossilized remains of tiny creatures that lived hundreds of millions of years ago. Each fossil is a work of art in its own right.

This is an ideal site to introduce someone to fossil hunting. Fossils are quite common, and you don't have to do any digging to find them. The richest deposits are found in the washout along the roadbed and the upper side of the road cut. Some fossils will be embedded in the soil, and they are easily dislodged with the aid of a trowel. Most crinoids, however, can be simply plucked from the ground.

One of the best times to go is after a rain. With each passing shower, new sea lily stems are exposed. In addition, the pelting raindrops erode the exposed soil, causing the buttonlike crinoids to wash downhill. Consequently, one of the best places to look for them is at the base of the exposed banks.

The most common fossils found will be individual crinoid disks. However, don't be surprised if you find a section of a sea lily stem with several segments still attached to one another. Also, be on the lookout for pieces of fossilized coral and brachiopods (clamlike shells 1 to 2 inches long).

Food and lodging: At exit 128 off I–75, there are five motels and a RV park along with more than half a dozen restaurants.

For more information:
The Georgia Geologic Survey
19 Martin Luther King Jr. Drive, Room 400
Atlanta, GA 30334
(404) 545–3214

The Nation's Champion Blackjack Oak

*This quiet churchyard boasts an enormous blackjack oak, leaving
visitors to wonder about the tree's history.*

Recommended time: October.

Name and location of site: Byron United Methodist Church, 14
miles (twenty minutes) south of Macon.

Minimum time commitment: One-half hour.

What to bring: Camera, field guide to trees.

Admission fee: None.

Directions: In Byron, at the junction of I–75 (exit 46) and SR 49, travel
east 0.8 mile to the junction of SR 42. Turn right and proceed 0.3 mile to
the Byron United Methodist Church on your right.

The background: You don't have to travel to the redwood and sequoia
forests of the western United States to see a big national champion tree.
Eighteen national champion trees grow in Georgia, and one of the most
unlikely of these is a blackjack oak growing in a quiet churchyard in Byron,
Georgia.

The blackjack oak is a small tree that rarely exceeds a height of 20 feet or
1 foot in diameter. The national champion tree growing beside the Byron
United Methodist Church has soared to 89 feet tall and has a circumference
of 11 feet.

Blackjack oaks range from northern Florida and north to southern New
York and New Jersey, west to Oklahoma and Nebraska, and south to Texas.
This hardy tree does well in poor, sandy, dry soil types that are inhospitable

to most trees. Here, this slow-growing tree produces acorns that are eaten by a variety of wild animals such as squirrels, turkeys, and deer.

The fun: When you stand at the base of this impressive tree and realize that it is the largest blackjack oak in the world, it is hard not to feel a sense of wonder. What caused this ancient oak to grow so much bigger than all others of its kind? Did man plant the tree decades ago? We will never know the answers to these perplexing questions.

Dendrologists (people who study trees) tell us that there are fifty-eight species of oaks native to North America north of the Mexican border. Using a field guide, take a few minutes and see if you can discover what features make the blackjack oak different from all other oaks.

A good place to begin your investigation is to look at its bark. It is very dark and split into squares. Next, turn your attention to the tree's leaves. They are 4 to 10 inches long, narrow at the base, and much broader at the tip. The leaf margins usually have three lobes and look very much like the webbed foot of a duck or goose or even the cross section of a pear. The tops of the leathery leaves are shiny. When you turn the leaf over, you will find it colored yellow or brown. By running your finger over the underside of the leaf you will discover that it feels hairy to the touch.

Look about the churchyard for fallen leaves and acorns. They make great mementos of a visit to this special tree.

Food and lodging: More than a half dozen motels and restaurants are within 2 miles of the tree.

For more information:

If you would like more information about the world-champion blackjack oak or The Georgia Champion Tree Program, contact:
Willard Fell
Georgia Forestry Commission
18899 US Highway 301 North
Statesboro, GA 30461
(912) 681–5347

Becoming a Tree Hunter

The blackjack oak beside the Byron United Methodist Church is but one of 177 state champion trees recognized by Georgia's Big Tree Program. Eighteen of these extraordinary trees are also national champions.

The registry of the largest trees found in the United States began in 1940. *American Forests Magazine,* the Davey Tree Expert Company, and Global ReLeaf 2000 sponsor the contest. The Georgia Forestry Commission administers Georgia's Big Tree Program.

A total of 823 species of naturalized and native trees are eligible for national records. The trees listed in the *1998–99 National Register of Big Trees* include the heaviest living organism in the world, a giant sequoia named General Sherman. It has been estimated that this mammoth tree weighs 6,167 tons. This tree is still growing although it is more than 3,800 years old. The largest pecan tree found in the United States grows in Weatherford, Texas. The crown of this nut-bearing tree is so broad that seven tennis courts could be placed beneath its spreading branches.

The tallest tree on the Georgia Big Tree List is an eastern white pine that towers 193 feet tall. This magnificent tree grows near Clayton in Rabun County. The tree with the biggest circumference is a live oak found in Waycross (Ware County). This record tree measures 407 inches (33.92 feet) around.

National champions have never been nominated for 136 species. Here in the Peach State, seventy-one species of trees known to grow in Georgia don't have champions. Georgia trees that have no state or national champions include American viburnum, bayberry, possumhaw, evergreen buckeye, pin corkwood, painted cherry, little snowbell, and silver bell.

Sadly, only five of the trees placed on the national registry during its first decade are currently listed. Trees succumb to disease, wind, lightning, and vandals.

Champion trees are determined by calculating point values. A tree's score is determined by adding its circumference in inches to one quarter of the average crown spread (in feet) and its height in feet.

Hunting for possible state and national champion trees is a great pastime for the whole family. Record trees can be found in backyards, along city streets, or in forests. All it takes to find one of these special trees is a keen eye. Before you begin your search, obtain a copy of the guidelines for nominating a tree in Georgia's Big Tree Program. With a little luck, you may soon be recognized as the discoverer of a new national or state champion tree.

30

A Visit to a Big-City Wetland

A small oasis deep in the big city lets visitors get lost in the wonder of wetland wildlife.

Recommended time: From October through May the Wetlands Center is open from 8:30 A.M. to 5:00 P.M. Wednesday through Sunday. From June through September the facility is open from 8:30 A.M. to 7:00 P.M. Wednesday through Friday and from 8:30 A.M. to 5:00 P.M. Saturday and Sunday.

Name and location of site: The Wetlands Center of the Clayton County Water Authority, 19.5 miles (thirty-two minutes) south of Atlanta.

Minimum time commitment: Two to three hours.

What to bring: Binoculars; field guides to birds, animal signs, and plants; camera. Pets are not allowed.

Admission fee: None.

Directions: From Atlanta: From the junction of I–20 and I–75, travel south on I–75 to US 41 (exit 235). Turn right onto Tara Boulevard. Drive 6.5 miles on Tara Boulevard to the junction of Freeman Road. Make a left turn onto Freeman Road and travel 0.8 mile to the Wetlands Center, which is on the right side of the road.

The background: The Wetlands Center is operated by the Clayton County Water Authority. Since 1995 the thirty-two-acre center has heightened appreciation of the value of wetland habitats to humans, wildlife, and plants. The facility is composed of a wetland education building, exhibits, and a 0.5-mile barrier-free trail that winds its way through and around a dynamic

Wetlands

Wetlands are habitats where the soil is saturated with water for part of the year. Some wetlands are wet only during certain periods, while others are always wet.

Wetlands are havens for wildlife. Two hundred species of fish and 150 different birds use our nation's wetlands. About 75 percent of our rare and endangered wildlife species use wetlands at some time during the year. This is an astounding number when you consider that wetlands make up only 5 percent of our country's land.

Historically, our failure to realize the importance of wetlands led to their abuse and destruction. At the time the first wooden ships laden with European settlers dropped anchor along the North American coastline, what was to become the United States contained 215 million acres of wetlands. Since then we have systematically filled, drained, and otherwise destroyed or degraded more than 125 million acres of wetlands. Today approximately 48 percent of the nation's wetlands are found in the Southeast. Georgia alone has 5.3 million acres of wetlands.

Wetlands are among our most valuable habitats. Besides providing valuable habitat for wildlife and plants, they help recharge our water supply, act as filters that remove harmful chemicals, help with flood control, and provide recreational benefits for thousands of Americans.

wetland. Programs for school groups and guided tours for visitors are also available.

The complex is located on a small portion of the land managed by the authority to treat wastewater, which uses such methods as spraying treated wastewater on woodlands. These woodlands receive the equivalent of more than 100 inches of rainfall a year as a result of this practice.

More than 130 species of birds and scores of other animals have been seen in the area. Dozens of plants can also be viewed in and around the wetland complex.

The fun: The Wetlands Center is a great place to visit at any time of year. If you look at the Wetlands Center as a giant stage, with each visit and season a new play is acted out as you walk the trail that winds its way through the facility.

On each trip, the first thing that you should do is visit the central exhibit/learning lab area. The staff at the center can give you tips as to what to look for at that time of year. If you are a bird-watcher, you will particularly like the list of interesting birds seen at the center in the recent past. The staff updates this list whenever new sightings are reported.

The center houses many interesting displays and mounts of animals that inhabit the area. If you have time, take a few minutes and view the center's wetland video.

To the left of the entrance to the exhibit/learning lab, you will find an interesting display, a visual representation of the wingspans of many of Georgia's birds. It's fun to stand in the center of the display and stretch out your arms to see which bird's wingspan comes the closest to matching the distance between your outstretched hands.

Plants and animals abound in the woodlands adjacent to the wetlands.

The wetland trail is easy to walk. Along the trail are several benches and a water fountain. In addition, three covered areas are provided along the trail where you can escape a sudden shower or the hot summer sun. While most of the trail hugs the margins of the wetland, boardwalks at the upper and lower ends carry visitors over the wetlands. This allows you to view wetland plants and animals that might otherwise only be accessible by wading through the boggy habitat.

Signs erected along the trail identify and interpret various features, plants, and animals. If you visit the site with children, pick up a free copy of *A Guide to the Wetlands Trail for Young People* at the central exhibit/learning lab area. This pamphlet provides tips on things that young visitors should look for on their hike.

The Wetlands Center's staff conducts guided tours of the wetland for groups of ten or more individuals Wednesday through Saturday. Reservations for guided tours can be made by calling ahead. From June through August guided tours are conducted without reservations. Look for scheduled guided hikes listed on the bulletin board at the head of the trail.

The Atlanta Chapter of the National Audubon Society conducts bird walks during the spring and fall bird migrations. Information regarding special events, such as this, is also posted on the bulletin board.

If you want to have the best chance of seeing a variety of wildlife, walk the trail very slowly and quietly. Constantly be alert for movement, sounds, and tracks that might reveal the presence of a wild animal. Mammals are much more difficult to see than birds; however, with a little luck, you might spot a muskrat, beaver, otter, mink, or other mammals on your visit. Look for the beaver lodge beneath the boardwalk just past the first bridge. Beavers are most active at night; however, in places where they are not harassed by people, they are often quite active during the day. While you might not see the beavers that live here, you should see trees that they have gnawed.

Amazingly, the noises of the vast metropolitan area that envelops this tiny oasis are, for the most part, filtered out by the woodlands surrounding the center. It's easy to imagine that you are in rural Georgia, far from the city.

Food and lodging: A good selection of motels and restaurants is within 15 miles of the Wetlands Center.

For more information:

The Wetlands Center of the Clayton County Water Authority
2755 Freeman Road
Hampton, GA 30228
(470) 603–5606

31

Fall

The Tree that Owns Itself

*A property owner of more than 68 square feet, this white oak has a
unique history all its own.*

Recommended time: October.

Name and location of site: The Tree that Owns Itself, in Athens.

Minimum time commitment: One-half hour.

What to bring: Camera, small bag for collecting acorns.

Admission fee: None.

Directions: In Athens, at the junction of US 29 and Prince Street, turn
onto Prince Street and continue 1.1 miles to the junction of Broad Street. At
the junction of Prince and Broad Streets, turn left onto Broad Street and
drive 0.3 mile to Finley Street. Turn right on Finley. Continue 0.1 mile to
the junction of Dearing Street. You will find the tree in a small plot of land
surrounded by chains on your left. A commemorative historic marker identifies the tree.

The background: One of the world's most unique trees grows in a quiet
residential neighborhood close to the campus of the University of Georgia.
When you gaze at the tree, it looks no different than the millions of other
white oak trees that grow throughout eastern North America. What makes
this tree so special is not its size or age, but the fact that it owns the land on
which it grows.

This amazing story has its beginnings in the early part of the twentieth
century. As fate would have it, the tree grew in the front yard of Col. William

The Tree that Owns Itself

H. Jackson, who was a professor at the University of Georgia. It is said that the tree was something to behold. Its massive spreading branches gave it a stately air, and its foliage provided a shady refuge for the colonel on hot summer days.

Colonel Jackson was so appreciative of his magnificent oak that in his will he deeded the property within 8 feet of the tree's massive trunk to the tree itself. This deed has never been tested. However, to this day, the tree has never been assessed any taxes by the city of Athens.

The Tree that Owns Itself was toppled by a storm on October 9, 1942. The majestic oak was so loved by the residents of Athens that before it could be hauled away two days after it fell, much of it was cut up as souvenirs. Four years after the tree's untimely death, the Athens Junior Ladies' Garden Club replanted a sapling on the plot where the giant oak once stood. The sapling came from good stock as it sprouted from one of the acorns produced by Colonel Jackson's beloved tree.

Today, the second-generation Tree that Owns Itself has become a magnificent white oak and carries on as perhaps the only tree in the world that owns itself and the land in which it is rooted.

The fun: The best time to take a trip to this special tree is the fall. At this time of year the weather is pleasant and the tree drops its crop of acorns. Consequently, not only do you get a chance to see this very special tree, you also get the opportunity to take home a souvenir—a white oak acorn. If you plant this fast-germinating acorn, with a little luck you will have a seedling growing in your backyard that came from one of the world's most unique trees. A word of caution: Don't wait too long to make the trek to Athens. Gray squirrels, blue jays, and other species of wildlife that live near this white oak may haul away the acorns before you get there.

Food and lodging: Five motels and twenty-one restaurants are found within 1 mile of the tree.

For more information:
Athens Convention and Visitors Bureau
220 College Avenue, Suite 7
Athens, GA 30601
(706) 546–1805
or
The Athens Welcome Center
280 East Dougherty Street
Athens, GA 30601
(706) 353–1820

32

Fall

A Visit with Southbound Travelers

*A banding station that monitors the fall migration of songbirds
allows visitors to view warblers and migrants close up.*

Recommended time: Late September through early October.

Name and location of site: The Jekyll Island Banding Station, 84 miles
(one hour and thirty minutes) south of Savannah. (See map on page 74.)

Minimum time commitment: Two to three hours.

What to bring: Camera, field guide to birds, binoculars, insect repellent,
sunscreen, folding chairs, long pants, walking shoes, beverages, and snacks.

Admission fee: The daily entry fee is $3.00 per vehicle. A $4.00 daily
vehicle permit allows one reentry onto the island. Both three-day ($12) and
seven-day ($24) vehicle passes are available. Both of these permits provide
unlimited reentry privileges.

Directions: From Savannah: From the junction of I–16 and I–95, drive
south on I–95 for 69.6 miles to the junction of US 17 (exit 29). Turn left and
continue on US 17 for 5.4 miles to the junction of SR 520 (Jekyll Island
Road). Turn right onto Jekyll Island Road and travel east 6.5 miles to
Riverview Drive. Turn right onto Riverview Drive and continue 2.6 miles to
the junction of Beach View Drive. Turn right onto Beach View Drive and
continue 0.1 mile to the junction of Macy Lane. Park in the public parking
area provided on the right side of the road.

The background: The Jekyll Island Banding Station is situated on Jekyll
Island State Park, in the shrubby dunes at the south end of the island. The

Migrating birds are caught in the mist nets stretched between the shrubs growing in the dunes.

park is managed by the Georgia Department of Natural Resources's, Parks, Recreation, and Historic Sites Division.

The Jekyll Island Banding Station (JIBS) is the oldest continuously operating banding station in Georgia. This nonprofit organization was founded by licensed bird banders Don and Doris Cohrs.

Since its inception in 1978, JIBS has been banding birds as part of a long-range effort to monitor the fall migration of songbirds along the Georgia coast. In addition, the station serves as an outdoor classroom where individuals and school groups can learn about banding and the conservation of songbirds.

Each year, approximately 2,000 birds are captured, banded, and released at the station. Over the years more than 35,000 birds, representing more than 120 species, have been banded. On busy days, 200 or more birds may be banded. The most common birds banded include common yellowthroats, palm warblers, gray catbirds, red-eyed vireos, American redstarts, and black-throated blue warblers.

The birds are captured in mist nets. The term "mist net" comes from the

Bird Banding

Since the United States and Canadian governments began a cooperative bird-banding program in the 1920s, more than forty million birds have been banded in North America by licensed banders. These banders come from many professions, from scientists and doctors to postal workers and homemakers. With proper training, anyone can be a bander.

Roughly 5 percent of the birds banded in North America have been recaptured or recovered. However, rates of return vary tremendously between species. For example, while upwards of 30 percent of all goose bands are reported, less than one-tenth of 1 percent of small birds, such as robins, warblers, and sparrows are ever reported.

Biologists use the data provided by band returns in a variety of ways: It helps reveal the migratory pathways taken by birds as they move to and from their breeding and wintering grounds, provides information regarding the timing and speed of the movements of migratory birds, and determines how long birds of different species live as well as the age structure of their populations.

The famous nineteenth-century naturalist and painter John James Audubon was perhaps the first to band birds in North America. Audubon placed strands of silver wire around the legs of nestling phoebes. Today, bands are made from an aluminum alloy. Each band has a unique number, which allows wildlife researchers to identify each individual bird reported.

If you find a banded bird that has died, report it to the U.S. Fish and Wildlife Service, Bird Banding Laboratory, 12100 Beach Forest Road, Laurel, MD 20708-4037. Carefully remove the band and send it in with the following information: the location (nearest town or city) where the bird was found, the date recovered, and your name and address. Once your report has been processed, the banding lab will send you a certificate that will identify the species of bird, its age, and where it was banded.

very fine, mistlike material used to make the nets. Birds become entangled in these nets as they fly through the shrubby vegetation at the banding station. Upon capture the birds are carefully removed and brought to the banding area, where they are weighed, measured, identified, and released unharmed.

The fun: The day begins early at the banding station. Nets are unfurled at dawn, which is about 7:00 A.M. at this time of year.

Once you have parked your vehicle, follow the signs to the canopy-covered area that serves as the temporary hub of the banding operations.

Visitors can do as much or as little as they like. The volunteers working the station are more than willing to describe every step of the banding operation as well as provide helpful tips on bird identification.

Experienced helpers, called band aids, check the nets every fifteen to twenty minutes. During each check, birds are carefully removed from the nets, placed in cotton bags, and brought to the banding area. After the birds have been processed, they are released.

On your first visit to the site, it is best to spend some time becoming familiar with all of the various tasks involved in operating the station. Watch and listen as the banders work with the birds. Follow the folks that patrol the nets and remove the captured birds. Above all, don't be afraid to ask questions. The people running the station want you to understand what they are doing and why banding is important to the conservation of migratory songbirds.

After you are familiar with each step in the banding process, volunteer to assist the banders—they are more than willing to let you help. In practically no time, they will have you helping to remove birds from the nets and carrying them back to the banding tables. They will even let you release a banded bird. This is the best way to get a real feel for bird banding. You will quickly find that bird banding is hard work and yet still lots of fun.

One of the best parts of your visit is that you can view warblers and other migrants close-up. Being able to examine a hand-held bird allows you to observe subtle features of the birds' plumage, eyes, bill, feet, and legs that are impossible to see through binoculars.

Normally, banding operations wind down between 11:00 A.M. and noon as birds begin to curtail their movements. Since the banders work as long as birds are being captured, on other days banding will continue into the afternoon. No banding is done on rainy days.

The success of these fall banding efforts is linked closely to the weather. Long stretches of beautiful, rain-free weather make for great days on the beach but poor trapping. Banding is usually much better after a weather front has moved through.

Food and lodging: A number of motels and restaurants are within 2 miles of the banding station.

For more information:
Jekyll Island Banding Station
c/o Don and Doris Cohrs
P.O. Box 1908
Darien, GA 31305
(912) 437–3333

33

Fall

A Visit to a Glittering Goliath

Stone Mountain offers a rare blend of outdoor adventures and amusement-park experiences.

Recommended time: Fall (though open all year).

Name and location of site: Stone Mountain Park, 7.7 miles (eight minutes) east of Atlanta.

Minimum time commitment: Three to four hours.

What to bring: Camera, binoculars.

Admission fee: $6.00 parking fee. Each attraction has an additional fee.

Directions: From the junction of I–285 (exit 39B) and Stone Mountain Freeway (GA 78), travel east 7.7 miles to the Stone Mountain Park exit. Follow the exit ramp around to the East Gate entrance.

The background: A short drive east of Atlanta stands the world's largest granite outcrop. This dome-shaped rock is 825 feet tall and covers 538 acres. It has been estimated that this massive rock weighs more than 126 billion pounds.

Geologists believe that the mountain was formed between 250 and 300 million years ago when the North American and African continents collided, causing hot molten rock to surge upward. When the rock finally cooled about 230 millions years ago, it was some 6 miles below the surface of the earth. Since then, wind and rain have slowly eroded away the ground, eventually exposing the imposing granite monolith that is now visible. As impressive as this mountain of granite is, only a small portion of this rock is visible.

The exposed granite at Stone Mountain covers 538 acres.

Geologists say that a portion of North Carolina and half of Georgia rest on its base.

Native Americans were the first humans to view Stone Mountain. Remains of their settlements suggest that they occupied this area more than 5,000 years ago. They called it Lone Mountain and held special meetings atop the granite dome.

Spanish captain Juan Pardo and his forces were the first Europeans to see the mountain. Historical documents reveal that when he and his men saw the sparkling mountain they thought that it was encrusted with diamonds. For this reason he dubbed the granite outcrop Crystal Mountain. However, before he learned that the mountain's glittering appearance was caused by quartz and not diamonds, he and his band were chased from the area by Native Americans. It is believed that the mountain got its current name when an early settler, L. H. Tumlin, owned a farm there. His land was so rocky that he called it Stone Mountain.

Over the years, quarry operations have slowly gnawed away at the mountain. Rock taken from the mountain has been shipped throughout the world to construct buildings such as the U.S. Capitol, roads, bridges, and even the locks on the Panama Canal.

Today, quarry operations have long since been silenced, and the mountain sits amid a 3,200-acre park. The state park is one of the most visited attractions in Georgia, hosting four million or more visitors annually.

One of the main attractions in the park is the world's largest carving. This work of art was cut some 400 feet above the ground on the north face of the mountain. Covering three acres (larger than a football field), the carving depicts Jefferson Davis, Robert E. Lee, and "Stonewall" Jackson on horseback. The size of the carving is mind-boggling; receded 42 feet into the mountain, the masterpiece measures 90 by 190 feet. Lee's head alone is 15.5 feet high.

The fun: Stone Mountain Park has something for everyone. The park provides opportunities to enjoy museums, nature, hiking, bicycling, boating, and much more. While a trip to Stone Mountain is fun at any time of year, fall is especially great—temperatures are cooling down, humidity is low, crowds are at a minimum, and the hardwoods are changing colors.

Begin your adventure by exploring Stone Mountain itself. There are two ways to reach the top of Stone Mountain. Some may prefer to hike the 1.25-mile hiking trail, along which you will find interesting plants and see and hear chickadees, red-bellied woodpeckers, and many other birds that inhabit the park. Make note of the different kinds of plants and animals as you make your way to the summit.

You will also see many fascinating geological features along the way. Take particular note of the cracks in the granite rock. These are exfoliation joints and are the result of expansion caused by the pressure created when the mountain was thrust upward and pressure was released. The process caused large slabs of granite to separate from the mountain. When these flat sheets of granite exfoliate (slough off), they leave shallow depressions called solution pits, which fill with water and provide a harsh habitat for some extremely small animals called clam and fairy shrimp. When the pits fill with water in the spring or fall, the tiny shrimp hatch. These fragile adult shrimp feed and produce eggs for the next generation. When the pits dry up, all that remains are the drought-resistant eggs that will hatch the following year.

Other interesting features are the white lines that cross the trail. While many think the lines are painted on the rock, they are actually veins of quartz.

For those that don't want to make the arduous hike to the top of Stone Mountain, the Mountaintop Skylift is made to order. The skylift carries guests 825 feet up the mountain in Swiss cable cars. A highlight of any trip is passing close to the Confederate Memorial carving on the side of the mountain.

Regardless of how you reach the top of Stone Mountain, you will be rewarded with a fantastic view of the City of Atlanta and surrounding landscape.

Those that don't want to make the journey up the monadnock can appreciate it from its base. Good views of the mountain can be had at many locations. One of the best places is found near Memorial Hall. You can also take a leisurely ride on the park train, which takes visitors on a 5-mile trip around the entire mountain.

If you want to explore the area surrounding the mountain on foot, hike one or more of the nature trails that wind through the park. If you don't want to venture far from the park's roads, you can walk along the 15 miles of sidewalks that hug the access roads. If you are a bird-watcher, some of the best places to see birds are the hiking trail up the mountain, the dam overlook, and the nature garden trail.

Stone Mountain Park also houses a zoo and has batting cages, canoeing, golfing, miniature golf, bicycling, swimming, tennis, ice-skating, museums, and a lazer show. Separate fees are charged for each of the major attractions within the park.

Food and lodging: Two hotels, the Evergreen and Stone Mountain Park Inn, are within the park. At least eight additional motels are in the nearby city of Stone Mountain. The park also has a 441-site campground with campsites designed for tents and recreational vehicles and two restaurants and snack bars. Nearby, in the city of Stone Mountain, there are a number of other eating establishments.

For more information:
Stone Mountain Park
P.O. Box 778
Stone Mountain, GA 30086
(470) 498–5690 or (800) 317–2006

34

Black-Water Sentinels in Their Autumn Splendor

Tall, stately cypress trees decked out in cinnamon-colored leaves set against a backdrop of blue skies and jet-black water is an image you will long remember.

Recommended time: October through November.

Name and location of site: George L. Smith State Park, a little more than 15 miles from Metter.

Minimum time commitment: Two to four hours.

What to bring: Camera, binoculars.

Admission fee: Daily parking is $2.00 per vehicle; an annual Georgia ParkPass is $25. Discounts are available for senior citizens.

Directions: Just south of Metter, at the junction of I–16 (exit 104) and SR 23, turn left (north) on SR 23 and travel 16 miles to the junction of George L. Smith State Park Road, which is marked with a sign and an arrow indicating the location of the park. Turn right and continue 1.9 miles to the park entrance.

The background: Each autumn thousands of people flock to the Georgia mountains to enjoy the splendor of the fall foliage. The beauty of north Georgia at this time of year is so dazzling that Mother Nature's handiwork in other parts of the state is often overlooked. If fall color is what you are looking for, it can be found in south Georgia, too, where leaf peepers can enjoy the colors provided by trees and shrubs that are not found in the mountains, such as bald and pond cypress. One of the best places to enjoy the fall foliage show staged by cypress is at the George L. Smith State Park.

This state park is one of Georgia's loveliest. The recreation area encompasses a 412-acre millpond impounded in 1880. A historic covered bridge and gristmill sit atop the dam at the south end of the pond. Scattered down the length of the lake are thousands of broad-buttressed cypress trees.

Two canoe trails have been marked through the pond's watery cypress forest. The red trail traverses the center of the lake northward to US 80, and the blue trail winds its way along the eastern shore of the pond before intersecting with the red trail.

The bald and pond cypresses are deciduous conifers. In other words, they are trees that shed their needlelike leaves. The leaves of the bald cypress are flat, pale green, and arranged in a featherlike pattern. In comparison, pond cypress leaves are long, keeled, and arranged in a spiral around the branchlets. The knees of pond cypress also differ from those of the bald cypress. Bald cypress knees are sharp pointed while those of the pond cypress are dome-shaped. In fall, cypress leaves turn cinnamon brown and, along with its smaller twigs, are shed.

The bald cypress gets its name from having a naked (bald) crown in winter. It is considered to be the largest tree that commonly grows east of the Rocky Mountains. Some cypress trees have grown to a height of 145 feet. Today most "big" cypress trees are 65 to 135 feet tall.

At one time, finding bald cypress trees that were 1,000 years old or older was common. However, due to extensive logging during the past two centuries, it is difficult to find trees more than 200 years old. The oldest known living bald cypress in the southeastern United States is about 1,400 years old and grows in North Carolina.

The pond cypress is a much smaller tree, rarely exceeding 80 feet in height. While the bark of the bald cypress is thin and tight, the bark of the pond cypress is thick and loose. Pond and bald cypress trees will often interbreed, making identification of individual trees difficult.

The fun: When you drive up to the boat ramp at George L. Smith State Park, it is hard to believe that you have not stumbled across a Hollywood set. The beauty of the scene is breathtaking. Looking right, you will see an impressive covered bridge that spans the dam across Fifteen Mile Creek. North of the dam, the black waters of the lake stretch as far as the eye can see. A profusion of Spanish moss–draped cypress trees dot the lake's surface, giving the landscape an aura of mystery. The best way to explore this mysteri-

Cypress trees tower above the black water of the park's lake.

ous body of water is by canoe. You can either bring your own or rent one from the park for $5.00 an hour, $15 for four hours, or $20 for eight hours.

Soon after you embark on your adventure, you must decide whether to take the red or blue trail. Once that decision has been made and the boat landing is far behind, you will enter another world. Take time to study the cypress trees that surround you, and see if you can tell whether you are looking at pond or bald cypresses. Listen and look for wildlife. You never know what you will encounter on your journey; each trip is a unique experience.

Take special note that cypress knees are only found surrounding trees that grow in shallow water or along the back of the lake. Nobody knows for certain the functions of these knees. Some suggest that they aid the tree's respiration, while others feel that they help anchor the trees in moist soil.

Even those that initially find this watery world to be foreboding will soon be captivated by its unadorned charm. The sight of tall, stately cypress trees decked out in cinnamon-colored leaves set against a backdrop of blue skies and jet black water is something you will long remember.

Food and lodging: Four cabins and twenty-five tent and trailer sites are located in the park, and twelve restaurants and four motels are within 16 miles of the park.

For more information:
George L. Smith State Park
P.O. Box 57
Twin City, GA 30471
(478) 763–2759

35

Fall

The Fall Flight of the Cloudless Sulphur

The cloudless sulphur wings its way through this coastal landscape on its way south to Florida, providing a unique opportunity for those intrigued by butterflies.

Recommended time: Late October.

Name and location of site: Jekyll Island, less than 15 miles from Brunswick. (See map on page 74.)

Minimum time commitment: One to two hours.

What to bring: Binoculars, sunscreen, insect repellent, field guides to butterflies and birds.

Admission fee: $3.00 per vehicle. A $4.00-per-vehicle permit allows you to reenter the island once. A three-day vehicle pass costs $12, and the seven-day pass is $24. Both provide unlimited reentry privileges.

Directions: At the junction of I–95 (exit 29) and US 17 south of Brunswick, turn left and continue 5.4 miles to the junction of Jekyll Island Road. Turn right on Jekyll Island Road and continue 6.9 miles until the road dead-ends at Beach View Drive. Turn right and travel south 1.5 miles to the soccer complex on your left. Park and walk the boardwalk out to the beach.

The background: While most people are familiar with the fall migration of the monarch butterfly, few realize that other insects also migrate. Some dragonflies, leafhoppers, moths, and other butterflies are also known to migrate. These migrations are different from those of birds because most insects' migratory movements are one-way. Rarely do the insects that migrate south in the fall, for example, return in the spring. If the members of that species do return, they are usually the progeny of the insects that made the southward flight.

The cloudless sulphur is a medium-size, showy butterfly that can be seen throughout the year. They measure from 2.25 to 3.8 inches long. Female cloudless sulphurs range in color from yellow to white, and the outer edges of their wings are bordered in black. The upper forewings sport a dark spot. The dorsal surfaces of the males' wings are lemon yellow. The lower hind-wings of both males and females are adorned with two pink-edged silver spots.

Some cloudless sulphurs that overwinter can be seen flitting about on warm winter days. In late summer, many cloudless sulphur butterflies begin to migrate southeastward. The migration is particularly evident along the Georgia coast, where thousands of cloudless sulphurs can be seen along Jekyll and other barrier islands. These travelers are heading toward Florida, where they will mingle with cloudless sulphurs raised there.

A morning spent on the beach during the migration will give you the opportunity to see more cloudless sulphurs than you would in your backyard during a lifetime of butterfly-watching.

The fun: While you are likely to see cloudless sulphurs anywhere along the beach, one of the best places to observe this mass migration is along the south end of the island. Park in the parking lot next to the soccer fields and take the boardwalk across the dunes.

Air temperature determines the time of day you need to begin your adventure. Butterflies are most active when temperatures range between 85 and 100 degrees Fahrenheit. If the temperature dips below 85 degrees, look for cloudless sulphurs that are basking.

Butterflies are cold-blooded, which means they cannot regulate their body temperature the way we do. Their body temperature is determined by the temperature of the surrounding air. In order to soak up the most heat, butter-flies expose their wings to the sun, which is called basking. Most butterflies bask by opening their wings so that the upper surfaces face the sun. However, cloudless sulphur butterflies bask in a different manner: They close their wings and expose their undersides to the sun.

Butterfly-watching is much like bird-watching. Binoculars allow you to study butterflies from a distance, but one problem that many butterfly-watchers have encountered is that most binoculars don't allow you to focus on a butterfly that is only a few feet away. However, some binocular manufacturers are now making close-focusing binoculars with butterfly-watchers in mind.

Begin your quest by scanning the landscape for butterflies. Usually, you will find cloudless sulphurs flying fairly close to the ground. Cloudless sulphurs are very strong flyers that steadily flap their wings; they do very little gliding.

Walk along the edge of the beach and sand dunes to the right of the end of the boardwalk. This will lead you to the south end of the island. When returning to the boardwalk, walk along the edge of the water. This will give you an excellent opportunity to beachcomb. Sometimes you will find the bodies of cloudless sulphurs washed ashore, mute testimony that many of these colorful insects never complete their migration.

If you encounter flocks of resting birds, give them a wide berth. Continual flushing of migratory shorebirds can be harmful, forcing them to abandon an area and expend energy needed to complete their migration.

As you look for cloudless sulphurs, keep your butterfly field guide handy. Chances are good that you will spot gulf fritillaries and a host of other butterflies that inhabit the island. At times groups of twenty to twenty-five dragonflies can also be seen winging their way southward.

Food and lodging: A large selection of motels and restaurants is within 2 miles of the site.

For more information:
Jekyll Island Welcome Center
P.O. Box 13186
Jekyll Island, GA 31527
(877) 4JEKYLL (toll-free)

36 *Fall*

Falling Leaves and Cascading Waters

*The tallest waterfall east of the Mississippi River is all the more
brilliant when framed in fall foliage.*

Recommended time: October.

Name and location of site: Amicalola Falls State Park, approximately
15 miles from Dawsonville.

Minimum time commitment: Two hours.

What to bring: Binoculars, camera, walking shoes.

Admission fee: Daily parking is $2.00 per vehicle; an annual Georgia
ParkPass is $25. Discounts are available for senior citizens.

Directions: In Dawsonville, turn left onto SR 53 and drive 2.6 miles to
the junction of SR 183. Turn right on SR 183 and continue 10 miles to the
junction of SR 52 and SR 183. Turn right on SR 52 and drive 1.5 miles to
the park entrance on the left.

The background: Amicalola Falls is the tallest waterfall east of the
Mississippi River. Here the rushing waters of Little Amicalola Creek noisily
plunge 729 feet, flow onward to join the Etowah River, and then gently proceed to the Gulf of Mexico, hundreds of miles to the south. In comparison,
the more famous American and Horseshoe Falls on the Niagara River are
173 and 182 feet high, respectively.

In addition to its impressive height, Amicalola is one of the country's most
breathtaking falls, situated along the slopes of a beautiful, mature southern
Appalachian cove forest. In this cathedral-like setting, the rushing waters of

Little Amicalola Creek rush over a series of seven cascades, creating a stunning stair-step effect.

The falls is nestled in the 1,023-acre Amicalola Falls State Park, which is located along the edge of the Blue Ridge Mountains. It is one of the most popular parks in the state, offering guests opportunities to watch wildlife, view wildflowers and fall foliage, hike, photograph nature, picnic, and fish for trout.

Eleven hiking trails wind through the park and vary from being wheelchair accessible to strenuous. The Fitness Trail has more than twenty exercise stations along its 1-mile length.

Special events and programs are offered throughout the year, including backpacking clinics and trips, October foliage display, and a special Sssnakes Alive program.

The top of the highest waterfall east of the Mississippi River

The fun: Picking one season as the best time to visit the falls is difficult—each season has its own allure. During March and April the water flow over the falls is greatest. During spring and summer an amazing array of wildflowers festoons the forest floor. In the autumn the woodlands are ablaze with fall foliage, and in winter the leafless trees reveal the best view of the falls.

Arguably, the falls is most beautiful in autumn, when it is framed in red, orange, crimson, and gold foliage. The array of colors creates an indescribable accent for the cataract that plummets more than 0.8 mile down the steep wooded slope.

The falls can be best viewed from two trails. The Base of the Falls Trail, which is 0.3 mile long and begins beside the reflecting pool, provides the best view of the falls. There is a small, often crowded parking lot nearby. The falls can also be viewed from a distance from the north end of the 1-mile-long East Ridge Trail.

The Falls Overlook can be reached two ways. You can take the East Ridge

Spring Trail (1.3 miles), whose trailhead is located behind the visitors center, or you can take a 0.4-mile trail loop near the parking lot close to the Amicalola Falls Lodge Conference Center. After an easy hike, visitors are rewarded with a panoramic view of the falls and surrounding countryside.

The falls is as dangerous as it is beautiful. Over the years eleven people have lost their lives when they left the trail and observation platforms for up-close views of the falls. With this in mind, the State Parks and Historic Sites Division strictly enforces regulations that require guests to stay on the trail in this hazardous area.

After visiting the falls, take a few minutes to wander through the exhibits in the visitors center. These displays interpret the fascinating natural history of the area.

Amicalola is the Cherokee word for "tumbling waters," the perfect term to describe the falls, one of Georgia's Seven Natural Wonders.

Food and lodging: A fifty-seven-room lodge, a restaurant, and eighteen tent, trailer, and RV sites are in the park. A least a dozen restaurants and overnight accommodations are within 20 miles of the park.

For more information:

Amicalola Falls State Park
418 Amicalola Falls Lodge Road
Dawsonville, GA 30534
(706) 265–8888

37

Fall

White-tailed Deer Abound at Red Top Mountain

This park allows visitors to view white-tailed deer from a surprisingly short distance and see the popular big game in its different seasonal attire.

Recommended time: Fall (however, viewing white-tailed deer is excellent year-round).

Name and location of site: Red Top Mountain State Park, 28 miles (thirty-five minutes) west of Atlanta.

Minimum time commitment: One hour. While deer can be seen throughout the day, they are most active early in the morning and late in the afternoon.

What to bring: Binoculars, camera.

Admission fee: Daily parking is $2.00 per vehicle; an annual Georgia ParkPass is $25. Discounts are available for senior citizens.

Directions: From Atlanta: From the junction of I–75 and I–285 in west Atlanta, drive north on I–75 for 26.4 miles to Red Top Mountain Road (exit 285). Head east on Red Top Mountain Road for 1.3 miles to the entrance of Red Top Mountain State Park.

The background: Less than an hour away from Atlanta, Red Top Mountain State Park is one of the most visited state parks in Georgia. The park encompasses a 1,950-acre peninsula surrounded on three sides by Lake Allatoona. The park's mixed pine-hardwood forest and miles of meandering

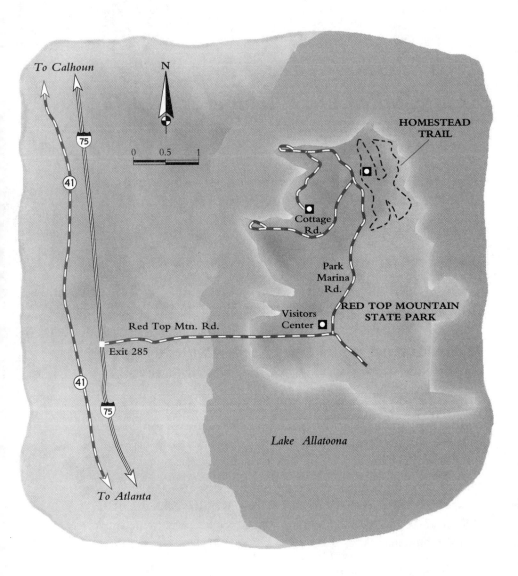

To Calhoun

N

75

41

0   0.5   1

HOMESTEAD TRAIL

Cottage Rd.

Park Marina Rd.

RED TOP MOUNTAIN STATE PARK

Red Top Mtn. Rd.

Visitors Center

Exit 285

41

75

To Atlanta

Lake Allatoona

shoreline provide visitors with panoramic vistas and the perfect setting for a variety of outdoor activities, including wildlife-watching, nature photography, hiking, camping, and picnicking.

The fun: Red Top Mountain State Park offers a wonderful opportunity to study deer in their natural wild habitat. White-tailed deer can be viewed either from a vehicle or while walking the 11 miles of foot trails that wind through the park. The easiest way to spot a deer is to drive slowly through the park while scanning the woodlands along the road. Do not attempt to view deer from Red Top Mountain Road, which is a busy highway—slowing down to look at deer could result in an accident.

In the fall and winter, some of the best spots to watch deer are at the designated wildlife-viewing areas along Cottage and Park Marina Roads. Here you can watch deer feeding on planted food patches from the comfort of your car. The deer have become acclimated to humans; consequently, they are quite tolerant of your presence. Therefore, have your camera ready as you should be able to get some excellent close-up shots of these normally wary creatures.

If you visit the park during different seasons of the year, the first thing you will notice is that the deer have two distinctly different coats. From spring through early fall, deer are reddish brown, and during fall they begin to replace their summer pelage with grayish winter coats.

Look for fawns from the late spring into early fall. They will have a row of white spots running down either side of their backbones and a hundred or so other spots scattered along each side of their bodies. These spots camouflage the young animals when they are curled up on the ground, helping them to blend into the pattern of spots of sunlight on the forest floor.

Look for antlers. Adult male deer, called bucks, grow antlers, and does (females) do not. If you visit the park in January or February, don't be surprised if you spot a buck with a single antler. It is not that unusual to see a buck in this condition as they will often shed each antler days apart. Once both antlers are lost, it is easy to mistake a buck for a doe. However, if you carefully look at the head of a buck, you will see what appears to be two round scars. In a short time, a new set of antlers will emerge from these.

Throughout the spring and summer, the antlers continue to grow. On visits to the park at these times of year, you will notice that the antlers appear to be very thick and covered with soft velvet, which carries blood to the growing antlers. When the antlers stop growing in late summer, the bucks will rub their antlers against small trees to remove the velvet.

Two does search for food.

As you drive through the park, you will probably notice that you can see far into the woods. This is because the few leafy plants are growing on or near the forest floor. In addition, most of the small branches of the trees are pruned up to about 7 feet above the ground. This phenomenon is called a browse line, which is about as high as a buck can reach when standing on its hind legs. Browse lines are only seen where deer populations are extremely high. The vegetation that remains lush below the browse line includes plants that deer don't like to eat.

Food and lodging: A restaurant, lodge, eighteen cabins, and campgrounds are in the park. A number of restaurants and motels are situated within a 10-mile radius of the park.

For more information:

Red Top Mountain State Park
781 Red Top Mountain Road SE
Cartersville, GA 30121
(470) 975–0055

38

Nature's Engineer

A quiet, patient wildlife-watcher may view the elusive beaver in its habitat.

Recommended time: November.

Name and location of site: Gordonia-Altamaha State Park, slightly more than a mile from Reidsville.

Minimum time commitment: One to two hours.

What to bring: Binoculars.

Admission fee: Daily parking is $2.00 per vehicle; an annual Georgia ParkPass is $25. Discounts are available for senior citizens.

Directions: From Reidsville take US 280 and go 1 mile to the junction of Park Lane and US 280. Turn onto Park Lane and drive 0.3 mile to the park.

The background: The beaver is truly a remarkable animal. With adults measuring up to 49 inches long and tipping the scales at sixty pounds or more, it is the largest rodent native to North America.

The beaver's ability to build dams and impound water has earned it the title of Nature's Engineer. These dams can be 1 to 10 feet high and vary in length from a few feet to hundreds of feet. The ponds created by the beavers' dam offer the animals safety as well as a means to transport food and building materials to their lodge.

While beavers' dam-building and feeding habits sometimes cause problems for humans, these activities actually do more good than harm. Beaver dams help control erosion, trap sediment, store water, and help control floodwaters, and they are some of our richest wildlife habitats, creating homes for a wide variety of birds, mammals, fish, reptiles, amphibians, and invertebrates.

Beavers are found throughout Georgia—in its largest cities, on farms, in swamps, and in wooded streams. In spite of the fact that they are so widespread, beavers are rarely seen. To see one, you have to be extremely lucky or very cautious.

The fun: Spotting a beaver will be a real challenge. While beavers are large, they are secretive and difficult to observe in the wild. To stand a chance of seeing one, your best strategy will be to arrive at the park an hour or two before sunset. Go immediately to the wetland colonized by the beaver, which is located just beyond the group shelter.

Park your car and walk down to the edge of the wetland. Here you will find two areas designated for viewing the beaver pond and lodge. One area provides an excellent view of the wetland. Scattered trees, shrubs, and other plants are interspersed with open water. This makes an ideal area for beavers to feed and collect building materials. At a second site an observation deck extends out into the wetland, and the beaver lodge can be viewed from here.

After you've had an opportunity to see the lodge and the pond from the two viewing areas, spend some time looking for beaver sign. Beaver tracks will be difficult to find; however, chances are good that you will find cuttings, trails, and scent mounds.

Scent mounds are nothing more than piles of mud and plants located along the shoreline. They are most often found in spring but can also be seen less frequently in fall. Beavers mark these sites with a pungent liquid called castoreum. Experts are not sure why beavers use scent mounds, but popular theories suggest that they are used to mark territories or that they play a role in mating.

Many animals chew bark, but the beaver is the only animal that leaves behind piles of wood chips. Check the trees and shrubs along the shore for signs of beaver usage. Also, scan the water for short logs cut by beavers. When beavers fell trees that are too large to carry, they will cut branches and trunks into smaller pieces that they can handle. After stripping the bark off these chunks of wood, they will either incorporate them into their dam or house or leave them floating in the pond. Beavers don't actually eat wood; however, they do dine on the soft inner bark of woody plants. Be on the lookout for trails leading away from the water. These trails can be up to a foot and a half wide and often lead to areas where trees and shrubs are cut.

Beavers are most active from early evening to dawn. However, in areas

A beaver's handiwork

where they are not harassed they can be seen moving about during the day. Therefore, as the sun begins to set, you should make preparations to begin your beaver watch.

To be successful, you must be extremely quiet and avoid sudden movements. While it is possible to spot a beaver from the observation deck, the fact that the deck is very close to the lodge lessens your chances tremendously. Most people can't stay still and silent long enough not to spook a beaver as it leaves its lodge to begin its nightly chores.

A better approach would be to sit in a lawn chair placed in front of a tree growing alongside the pond. The tree will help conceal your outline. In addition, the impact of any sounds and motions will be lessened.

As you sit and wait, scan the surface of the pond for any movement. Your first glimpse of a beaver will probably be a dark head moving steadily through the water. If there is more than one beaver, compare the size of each head. As you might expect, younger beavers have smaller heads. If you are lucky, you may even see a beaver carrying a stick back to its lodge. If the beavers don't detect your presence, they may even leave the water in search of food. However, if they sense danger, you will hear a large splash, which is caused by the alarmed beaver slapping its tail against the water. This is a warning signal to all the beavers in the colony that danger is near. If you hear such a splash, don't move; the beavers may have detected sound in the nearby woodlands or seen a large bird fly overhead. Once satisfied that the perceived threat has passed, the animals may resume their normal activities.

Although spotting a beaver is not easy, if you are successful, you can return home filled with the pride of knowing that you practiced good outdoor skills.

Food and lodging: Twenty-six tent, trailer, and RV sites are available at the park. A number of restaurants and motels are in Metter, 23 miles away. There are also restaurants in Reidsville.

For more information:

Gordonia-Altamaha State Park
P.O. Box 1039
Reidsville, GA 30453
(912) 557–7744

39

Mother Nature's Fall Show

Georgia's mountain landscape cloaked in vibrant fall foliage is best viewed from this scenic drive.

Recommended time: The last weekend in October.

Name and location of site: Richard B. Russell Scenic Parkway, just outside of Helen.

Minimum time commitment: Four hours.

What to bring: Camera, binoculars, field guide to trees.

Admission fee: None.

Directions: In Helen, take GA 356 for 2.3 miles to the junction of GA 348 (Richard B. Russell Scenic Parkway) and begin your tour.

The background: One of the most eagerly awaited natural events of the year is the annual fall foliage show. While this annual pageant can be viewed in all parts of Georgia, it is most dramatic in the mountains. Travelers visiting this region at just the right time can enjoy scenic vistas accented with a kaleidoscope of breathtaking colors.

The fun: One of the most spectacular mountainous fall foliage shows can be seen along the 13.4-mile Richard B. Russell Scenic Parkway. Here you can leisurely drive along the winding road and enjoy Mother Nature's handiwork. Most folks, however, prefer to pull off the road into one of the many turnoffs located at particularly scenic overlooks, where you can view the colorful foliage at your own pace. Others stop at the two well-marked points where the Appalachian Trail crosses the parkway and make a short trek along

In autumn, the hillsides along the highway are blanketed in a multihued quilt of fall colors.

this famous walking path. This provides the opportunity to savor the earthy scent of the fall woodlands and listen to the sound of dry leaves crunching beneath your feet.

Short trips into the woodlands also offer the chance to study fallen leaves up close. Examples of these leaves can be placed in top-loading polypropylene sheet protectors and stored in a three-ring binder for later identification and enjoyment.

Veteran leaf peepers can identify distant trees simply by their fall colors. Each tree has its own special colors and leaf shape. Here is a list of the colors of the fall foliage of some of the trees you will see:

Beech: yellow to bronze
Black cherry: greenish yellow
Black gum: red
Flowering dogwood: red
Hickory: golden yellow
Hop hornbeam: bright yellow
Ironwood: orange to red

Red and white mulberry: yellow
Red maple: bright orange, red, occasionally yellow
Redbud: greenish yellow
River birch: yellow to brown
Sassafras: yellow to red and orange
Scarlet oak: bright scarlet
Sourwood: red
Sumac: orange, red to yellow
Sweetgum: salmon, maroon, red, orange to yellow
Tulip poplar: golden yellow

Whichever way you choose to enjoy this eye-popping outdoor show, you will return home with a treasure trove of stunning images stored in your memory and on film.

Food and lodging: There is a wide range of dining and overnight accommodations in Helen.

For more information:

U.S. Forest Service
Chattahoochee-Oconee National Forest
508 Oak Street NW
Gainesville, GA 30501
(470) 536–0541
U.S. Forest Service Leaf Watch Hotline:
(800) 532–2521
Georgia Department of Industry, Trade, and Tourism:
(800) 847–4842

How Do Leaves Change Color?

Mother Nature doesn't paint her multihued fall mural by simply sweeping her magical brush across the north Georgia mountains at the first sign of frost. Like all great masterpieces, this work of art is the product of weeks of preparation.

This laborious process begins on June 21, the longest day of the year. On this, the Summer Solstice, Earth begins to slowly tip on its axis. As a result, our days become shorter. This affects plants that use sunlight to manufacture food. The chemical that permits plants to convert the sun's energy into food is called chlorophyll, and this pigment also gives leaves their green color. It is so abundant that it usually masks the other pigments found in leaves. As the sunlight available to plants wanes, plants use their precious chlorophyll faster than it can be replenished. Once it is exhausted and converted into colorless chemicals, the other colors that the chlorophyll has shrouded, such as yellow and orange, are visible.

Some plants convert their sugars and other chemicals into substances called anthocyanins. Since these compounds are red, once the chlorophyll in their leaves disappears, they are ablaze with hues of red, maroon, and orange.

The leaves of some trees, like many oaks, aren't cloaked with vibrant colors because their leaves contain huge amounts of tannin. As a result, they simply turn brown. A notable exception to this is the scarlet oak. Each autumn, its leaves are transformed from green to bright scarlet, making it one of the most attractive trees that adorns Georgia's woodlands.

The attractiveness and length of the annual fall-foliage extravaganza varies from year to year. Dry summers can result in intensified fall foliage, but on the downside, summer drought can result in leaves dropping early. In fall, balmy, sunny days accented with crisp nighttime temperatures also enhance leaf color. While a little bit of fall rain can help trees retain their leaves, heavy downpours accompanied by gusty winds can strip trees of their colorful cloaks.

40

Bedtime for Vultures

Watch turkey vultures on their way back to their lakeside roost in Reed Bingham State Park.

Recommended time: December through January.

Name and location of site: Reed Bingham State Park. The roost is 6.7 miles (fifteen minutes) east of Adel.

Minimum time commitment: Two hours.

What to bring: Binoculars, field guide to birds.

Admission fee: Daily parking is $2.00 per vehicle; an annual Georgia ParkPass is $25. Discounts are available for senior citizens.

Directions: From Adel and the junction of I–75 (exit 39) and SR 37, travel west on SR 37 for 6 miles to the junction of CR 99. Turn right on CR 99 and continue 0.3 mile to the junction of CR 221. Turn left on CR 221 and drive 0.4 mile to the park entrance.

The background: Both turkey and black vultures are found in Georgia. The black vulture is a true bird of the South since its range is centered in the southeastern United States, but it is seen as far north as Maryland and westward to Texas. While black vultures are considered nonmigratory, some do venture southward in winter.

The turkey vulture is far more cosmopolitan; its range spans much of the contiguous United States and southern Canada. Each fall, turkey vultures migrate southward in large flocks. Some of these migrants soar as far south as South America; however, in the eastern United States, most turkey vultures winter in Florida. Georgia hosts both resident and migrating turkey vultures in winter.

Both turkey and black vultures roost in groups. These nighttime roosts are usually much larger in winter. The number of birds using a winter roost can vary widely, and concentrations of 100 to 400 birds are common. The largest roosts may host upwards of 4,000 birds. Although black and turkey vultures will at times roost together, they usually roost apart.

One of Georgia's best-known winter turkey-vulture roosts is in Reed Bingham State Park. Each day through the winter turkey vultures converge on the park in late afternoon. The numbers of birds roosting here vary from year to year, with peak numbers recorded from December through February. The sight of large numbers of turkey vultures arriving or leaving a roost is impressive.

The fun: The two best times to observe turkey vultures at this roost are early morning and late afternoon. If you want to see the birds returning to the roost, plan to arrive at the park between 3:00 and 4:00 P.M. and to stay until after the sun sets. This will give you plenty of time to find some of the better vantage points from which to spot the arriving birds.

The birds predominantly roost at the north end of the lake, but also check out the fishing dock and the boat ramps situated on the east and west sides of the lake. Select a site, and then scan the horizon for arriving birds.

The birds arriving at the roost have been soaring over the south Georgia countryside all day searching for dead animals and other foods. With the proper wind conditions, they can soar for hours without flapping their wings, often reaching altitudes that range from 10,000 to 20,000 feet. Whether the birds glide or flap their wings to reach the roost depends on wind conditions. On windy afternoons, these large birds can wing into the roost with little effort. When winds are calm, they have to use more effort to reach their perches. Some vultures may cover 200 miles in a day's time.

In many ways, viewing a vulture roost in the morning is more exciting than an afternoon vigil. The light is better, and you can watch the birds' interesting behavior before they embark on the day's flight. Vultures are not early risers; turkey vultures usually don't begin leaving their roosts for more than an hour after the sun has risen. Vultures spend much of their time preening their feathers, stretching, and getting warm. They particularly like to hold their wings out so that they can catch the warming rays of the rising sun. They can also be seen stretching their wings and legs as well as flapping their wings.

Nature's clean-up crew at work

On foggy, rainy, or windless mornings, vultures stay on the roost until conditions are suitable for flying. The longer they stay, the less chance they will have of finding food that day. When the conditions are right, they lift off their perches and try to catch wind currents that will carry them aloft for a day of scanning the landscape for their next meal.

While watching for the vultures, keep a sharp eye out for other birds. It is not uncommon to see flocks of wood ducks and other waterfowl moving about.

Food and lodging: Eight motels and more than half a dozen restaurants are in Adel.

For more information:

Reed Bingham State Park
Route 2, Box 394B1
Adel, GA 31620
(229) 896–3551

41

Mustangs, Spanish Moss, and Seaside Legends

Ribbons of white-sand beaches that stretch to the horizon and Spanish moss–festooned live oaks highlight this sublime landscape.

Recommended time: December through January.

Name and location of site: Cumberland Island National Seashore, 105 miles (one hour and thirty-six minutes) south of Savannah.

Minimum time commitment: Eight hours.

What to bring: Backpack, food, beverages, insect repellent, sunscreen, camera, binoculars. No supplies are available on the island.

Admission fee: The day-use fee is $2.00 per person per day and $4.00 per person for ten days. An annual day-use pass is $20 per person. The Sea Camp Campground is $4.00 per person per day; backcountry camping is $2.00 per person per day. The ferry to the island runs daily from March through September and Thursday through Monday from October through February. Fares are $10.17 for adults, $8.03 for senior citizens (sixty-five and older), and $6.05 for children (twelve and younger).

Directions: In St. Marys, the visitors center is located just to the right of the intersection of SR 40 and St. Marys Street.

The background: The free-ranging horses on Cumberland Island are perhaps the most picturesque, destructive, and controversial animals that inhabit this tranquil barrier island. The horses share this island paradise with 325 species of birds and dozens of species of mammals, reptiles, and amphibians.

Cumberland Island, the southernmost barrier island along the Georgia coast, is 16 miles long and ranges from 0.5 to 3 miles wide. Its 17.5-mile beach is said to be the longest strand of unspoiled beach along the Atlantic Coast.

While the island has been designated a National Wilderness, the island's resources have been exploited by humans. Since the Colonial period, the trees that were part of a once virgin maritime forest have been cut for firewood and to build ships and cleared for raising indigo, cotton, and corn. Since these pursuits were abandoned decades ago, the land has been slowly healing itself. While signs of human intrusion can still be seen here, the beauty of the island is breathtaking.

The horses cannot really be considered wildlife; they are feral animals that have descended from domestic stock that escaped or were released. Popular legend suggests that their lineage extends back to Spanish horses brought to this county during the sixteenth century. These animals supposedly bred with Appaloosas obtained by former landowners from the King Ranch in Texas.

It is estimated that roughly 200 horses currently inhabit the island. This represents a 50 percent increase in the herd population during the past fifteen years. As the horse herd has increased, it has caused harm to the island's ecology. This is particularly true in the inter-dune area along the beach, where the horses have overgrazed sea oats and other plants that help keep the dunes from eroding away. The horses have also damaged the marsh grasses found on the western side of the island. Marsh grasses are the preferred food of the horses, who spend a lot of time grazing in the vast salt marshes.

Since the horses are extremely popular with the public, the National Park Service wants to maintain representative herds on the island, allowing people to see the horses that have become an integral part of a trip to Cumberland Island. However, in order to lessen the damage being done to the island's plant communities, the horse population must be reduced. The Park Service is currently evaluating humane ways to do this.

The fun: Your destination is a barrier island 3 miles off the coast of Georgia. Since no supplies can be purchased on the island, you must bring everything that you will need during your visit. Consequently, stock your backpack with all the beverages, food, sunscreen, and insect repellent needed for a day outdoors.

The Park Service allows only 300 people a day to visit the island. Therefore, you must call ahead to reserve a place on the ferry that will transport you to the island. Reservations are also required for overnight stays, and the Park Service accepts reservations eleven months in advance. It is always a good idea to make your reservations as soon as possible as daily visitation quotas are quickly met.

The ferry goes to and from the island twice a day. Departure times from the St. Marys dock are 9:00 A.M. and 11:45 A.M., and the boat returns to the mainland at 10:15 A.M. and 4:45 P.M. If you are visiting the island for the day and miss the late boat, you have to charter a boat to get back to St. Marys. From March 15 through September 30, the ferry also leaves the island at 2:45 P.M. No ferry service is provided on Tuesday and Wednesday from October 1 through March 14.

Before the ferry leaves for the island, visitors are given a brief orientation. Don't tune out the ranger giving the talk—the information offered can be a real help to you later in the day. The journey to Cumberland Island lasts about forty-five minutes and takes you down the Saint Marys River and across Cumberland Sound. Be on the lookout for dolphins, shorebirds, wading birds, gulls, terns, and other wildlife during the trip.

Upon arriving at the Dungeness Dock, another park ranger will offer additional information designed to make your day on Cumberland Island enjoyable. Take particular note of where you can obtain drinking water and the locations of the four rest room facilities.

Since you have to walk everywhere you go on Cumberland Island, concentrate your search for the wild horses on the south end of the island. Begin by making the short 1-mile walk from the Dungeness Dock to the beach. Horses are often seen loafing and feeding on the dunes. At times they will even wade out into the surf in order to escape mosquitoes and biting flies. As you walk across the dunes, you will see where the horses have closely cropped the vegetation, evidence of the damage being done by these intriguing animals.

If you are more adventuresome, take the 3.5-mile loop trail that leads to the seemingly foreboding Dungeness Ruins. This route then heads east to the beach. At the beach, head north to the Sea Camp Beach Campground, and then follow the trail west to Sea Camp Dock. You can board the ferry there or walk north along the River Trail to Dungeness Dock, where you began.

Whichever route you take, you are likely to see the horses practically anywhere. Aside from the inter-dune area, excellent places to see horses are along the edge of the salt marsh and near the remains of Dungeness, one of the most fascinating sites on the walk. All that remains of this stately mansion, which boasted sixteen fireplaces, are crumbling sections of the walls and

Wild horses contently graze on Cumberland Island.

chimneys. Walking through the skeletal remains of this once majestic mansion, it is easy to understand why legends of ghosts swirl around this isolated island. Next to the house, the remnants of a walled garden are a solemn reminder of a bygone era. Built by Thomas Carnegie during the 1880s, the mansion was used by the Carnegie family for decades. After years of disuse, the stately residence mysteriously burned in 1959.

The horses that you will encounter as you explore the island are usually segregated into groups. Each group or band consists of a stallion and his harem of mares and their colts. Since the stallion chases off the young stallions when they are about two years old, some groups will be composed of stallions that have not yet been able to assemble their own harems. While the animals are quite tame, for your own safety, don't try to approach them too closely.

Cumberland Island is a nature lover's paradise. It has one of the most diverse bird populations anywhere in Georgia. In winter, more than 140 species of birds can be seen, including bald eagle, peregrine falcon, northern gannet, common loon, wood stork, marbled godwit, dunlin, piping plover, golden-crowned kinglet, American pipit, yellow-throated warbler, tricolored heron, and many more.

In addition to the horses, some of the other mammals you are likely to spot are white-tailed deer, feral hogs, armadillos, and raccoons. Raccoons are quite common in the campgrounds; in fact, their propensity for pilfering food from campers has many believing that they deserve their black "robber" masks.

When you set foot on Cumberland Island, you enter another world, a place to relax and enjoy nature. As you stroll down Main Road beneath a living arch created by spreading live oaks festooned with Spanish moss, you'll feel that you are in a place where man is an interloper. Hopefully it will remain that way for generations to come.

Food and lodging: Camping is permitted on the island; call ahead to reserve a campsite. One inn is located on Cumberland Island, and more than a dozen restaurants are within 2 miles of St. Marys. In addition, more than a dozen bed-and-breakfast establishments and motels are within 10 miles of St. Marys.

For more information:

Cumberland Island National Seashore
P.O. Box 806
Saint Marys, GA 31558
(912) 882–4336 (information only) or (912) 882–4335 (reservations only)

42

Winter

Blackbirds Everywhere!

More than a million red-winged blackbirds choose this site as their
winter roost. Watch the flocks return after a day of foraging.

Recommended time: December through January.

Name and location of site: Crisp County blackbird roost, 61 miles
(one hour) south of Macon.

Minimum time commitment: One hour around sunset.

What to bring: Folding chairs, binoculars, camera equipped with high-
speed film, field guide to birds.

Admission fee: None.

Directions: Travel south on I–75 to the junction of I–75 (exit 99) and SR
300. Upon exiting I–75, turn right and take an immediate right at the RIDE
SHARE PARKING LOT sign.

The background: This large blackbird roost covers more than eight
acres, and the birds roosting here use two very different types of habitats.
Some roost in the bare branches of hardwood trees that border the fields and
highway right-of-way, while others prefer to spend the night in the dense
foliage of the eleagnus shrubs that blanket the slopes of the intersection's
access ramps.

It is estimated that some 200 million red-winged blackbirds and starlings
winter in the southeastern United States, roosting in flocks that vary tremendously in size. Some roosts contain fewer than a dozen birds, while others
contain upwards of thirty million birds. The Cordele roost is one of the

Thousands of blackbirds will roost in a single tree.

estimated 150 major blackbird roost sites scattered across the South. To be considered a major roost, a site must contain one million or more birds.

The fun: Plan to arrive at the roost about an hour before sunset, which will give you plenty of time to decide where you want to watch this remarkable wildlife spectacle. While you can view the birds' arrival from the Ride Share Parking Lot, visibility from there is somewhat limited because it is situated below the roadbeds of both I–75 and GA 300. Consequently, you might want to consider parking on the spacious shoulder of the road east of the I–75 overpass.

Once you have settled in, scan the horizon for flocks of blackbirds. Usually most of the birds will approach the roost from the north and west, arriving in flocks that range in size from fifty or fewer to several hundred. These birds have spent the day miles from the roost, foraging for food among the vast farmlands that form a quiltlike pattern in this, the agricultural heartland of Georgia.

As sunset approaches, long phalanxes of birds will stream toward you. Watch how some flocks seem to fly in a straight line toward the roost, and then note how many flocks don't directly fly to a roost, preferring instead to mill about as if trying to decide exactly where they will spend the night.

Birds of a Feather . . .

Although we commonly see flocks of birds, the sight of a flock of a million or more birds is an experience one long remembers. Flocking offers many advantages to the members of the flock. For example, a bird in a flock stands less of a chance of being caught by a predator than a bird living alone. Should a hawk try to catch a bird in a flock, it must keep its attention focused on a particular bird, which is often extremely difficult when birds are swirling about and trying to escape the hawk's sharp talons. Similarly, it is very difficult for a predator to approach a flock undetected. In a flock, thousands of eyes and ears are constantly on the lookout for danger.

Flocking also offers particular advantages to birds making their first migration. When young birds flock with adults that have previously migrated to and from nesting grounds, they are taught the best places to roost and feed. Without the benefit of the older birds' experience, the younger birds might have a difficult time finding these important habitats.

One disadvantage to being a member of a flock is that competition is often keen. Consequently, the best roosting and feeding sites often go to the older, more experienced birds. If a bird can't successfully compete with the other members of its flock, its chances of survival are slim.

Others blacken the fields next to the roosting areas, perhaps trying to feed once more before roosting for the night. Listen as the flocks noisily announce their arrival at the roost. As more flocks gather, the volume of the birds' raspy calls swells to an impressive level.

As the sun continues to sink slowly in the west, the number of birds arriving at the roost site increases and the birds urgently search for a suitable roosting spot. Flocks of birds form whirlwinds above the roosting site as they prepare to settle in for the night, and the branches of the leafless trees southeast of the intersection quickly fill with birds. The trees southeast of the intersection will appear to be festooned with thousands of blackened leaves. Other blackbirds prefer to roost in the thick cover created by the tangles of eleagnus bushes that cloak the steep banks of the intersection. The birds roosting in this area disappear as they dive into the rank vegetation.

The vast majority of the birds using the site are male red-winged black-birds. However, the redwings share the roost with other birds such as common grackles, brown-headed cowbirds, and starlings.

Male redwings are solid black with bright red shoulder patches, the trailing edges of which are bordered in yellow. Often only slivers of red and yellow are visible when the bird is perched. Female and immature red-winged black-birds are brownish and accented with dark streaks. Male redwings are slightly larger (9 inches long) than females (7 inches long).

If you'd like to keep a lookout for other bird species at the roost, note that female brown-headed cowbirds have a drab brown appearance. In comparison, male cowbirds have black bodies and brown heads. Cowbirds measure about 7 inches long. Starlings are chunky, dark birds. At a distance they will seem black; however, on close examination their plumage is marked with white spots. Starlings are roughly 8 inches long. The common grackle is the largest (12 inches long) bird that you will regularly see at this roost site. Although they are iridescent purple in color, they will appear black from a distance. Common grackles have long, wedge-shaped tails. Finally, look for hawks and owls, which are known to hunt here, taking advantage of the large blackbird population.

Food and lodging: More than two dozen restaurants and eight motels are within 5 miles of the site.

For more information:

Georgia Nongame-Endangered Wildlife Program
116 Rum Creek Drive
Forsyth, GA 31029
(478) 994–1438

43

Winter

Rafts of Sea Ducks

A closer-than-normal look at a 100,000-strong winter waterfowl concentration is possible from the northern shore of Jekyll Island.

Recommended time: Mid-November through January.

Name and location of site: Jekyll Island, approximately 15 miles from Brunswick. (See map on page 74.)

Minimum time commitment: One to two hours.

What to bring: Binoculars, spotting scope, field guide to birds.

Admission fee: The daily entry fee is $3.00 per vehicle. A daily $4.00-per-vehicle permit allows one reentry to the island. Both three-day ($12) and seven-day ($24) vehicle passes, which provide unlimited re-entry privileges, are available.

Directions: Just south of Brunswick, at the junction of I–95 (exit 29) and US 17, turn left (east) on US 17 and continue 5.4 miles to the junction of Jekyll Island Road. Turn right and travel east for 6.3 miles to the junction of Beach View Drive. Turn left on Beach View Drive and continue 3.2 miles to the picnic area on the right, just north of the Villas by the Sea.

The background: The largest concentrations of waterfowl in Georgia traditionally occur along the coast. However, since these large flocks are often 5 or more miles from shore, they are rarely seen. One of the best places to regularly see these birds from shore is the north end of Jekyll Island, where the birds often feed and loaf in large rafts. It is estimated that in late November and early December 1998, rafts of more than 100,000 birds were seen from this beach.

The birds that make up these flocks are primarily lesser scaup and black scoter, but there are also greater scaup, red-breasted merganser, surf scoter, white-winged scoter, and redhead. Besides the red-breasted merganser, which is a fish-eating duck, the other ducks feed primarily on the mussels, clams, and other aquatic invertebrates that live on the ocean bottom off the Georgia coast. These birds are capable of diving to depths of 40 feet or more in search of food.

The fun: This trip can be both challenging and extremely rewarding. Often the ducks are most abundant during blustery weather. While the birds have little difficulty riding the waves in such weather, it is extremely hard to study birds that are continually moving up and down on 4- to 5-foot swells as you try to steady your scope. By the same token, it is satisfying to find an unusual duck in a raft of ducks that numbers in the tens of thousands.

Since you will be attempting to study birds at great distances, you will need a spotting scope on this trip. Usually, a 20 to 40 variable power scope is ideal for this type of wildlife-watching.

Standing on the beach and looking out at a raft of ducks that seems to stretch out of sight can be a little overwhelming. When faced with this situation, one of the best ways to begin is to quickly scan all of the ducks, which will give you a good feel for the size of the flock and how many different species you are dealing with. You are then ready to methodically study the birds.

If you are unfamiliar with ducks, don't try to learn the field marks for all of the species illustrated in your field guide before making your trek to the coast. Instead concentrate on the seven aforementioned species that you are most likely to find. If you can learn to identify the males and females of just two species, you will be able to identify more than 90 percent of all the birds you are likely to see.

The most common duck seen here is the lesser scaup, and the male, which has a bright blue bill, is easy to identify. When floating on the ocean, they will seem black fore and aft with a broad white band around their bodies. The females are brown and have white patches at the base of their bills.

Although the greater scaup looks much like a lesser scaup, it is far less abundant on the Georgia coast. While there are a few subtle differences between the two birds, realistically, the only way that you can separate them is by studying their wings in flight. Although both have white stripes on the trailing edges of their wings, this stripe is much longer on the greater scaup.

The second most common duck in the area is the black scoter. The male black scoter is entirely black and sports a bright orange-yellow knob on the base of its bill. The female is a grayish brown bird with a darker crown and light cheeks.

When you first look at a large raft of ducks, you might think that it is impossible to accurately estimate how many birds you are looking at. Actually, it is not as hard as you might think. All you have to do is to count the number of ducks you see in a certain area, and then count how many areas of equal size the raft occupies. To get the total number of ducks, multiply the number of areas times the ducks counted in one area.

Food and lodging: More than a dozen restaurants and ten hotels are on the island, within 2 miles of the site.

For more information:

Georgia Nongame-Endangered Wildlife Program
1 Conservation Way
Brunswick, GA 31523
(912) 262–7355

44

The Christmas Bird Count:
A Holiday Tradition

Take part in this annual activity in Georgia's mountains and help count fifty or more species of birds.

Recommended time: The first Sunday of the count period (December 14–January 5).

Name and location of site: Chattahoochee National Forest–Songbird Management Area, a few miles from Chatsworth.

Minimum time commitment: Four hours.

What to bring: Field guide to birds, binoculars, snacks, and beverages.

Admission fee: $5.00 per participant.

Directions: From Chatsworth, at the junction of US 411 and SR 52, turn left onto SR 52 and proceed 2.1 miles to the junction of SR 52 and Old Ellijay Road. Continue on until you come to the U.S. Forest Service Office.

The background: The Christmas Bird Count, sponsored by the National Audubon Society, is the longest continuous survey of bird populations conducted anywhere in the world. Over the years, data collected during these counts have provided biologists with valuable information regarding the status of bird populations and the health of our environment. For example, counts have documented the spread of the house sparrow throughout the eastern United States and the expansion of the Eurasian collared dove across Georgia.

The count gets its name from the fact that it takes place during a two-and-a-half-week period around Christmas. Each year the counts are held in the same count circle, which is truly massive, measuring 15 miles in diameter (approximately 177 square miles).

The count rules are simple. Participants count and try to identify every bird they encounter during a single calendar day. Birds can be identified either by sight or their calls.

The first Christmas Bird Count was held on Christmas Day in 1900 with only twenty-seven people counting birds at twenty-five locations scattered across North America. The event was staged to give people an alternative to a popular holiday sporting event that pitted teams against one another to see who could shoot the most wildlife in one day. By 1998 the popularity of the Christmas Bird Count had swelled to the point where 1,767 counts were held throughout the United States, Canada, Mexico, Central and South America, and the Caribbean. These counts attracted 48,980 folks that tallied 57,976,634 birds.

The fun: Christmas Bird Counts are great fun for the whole family. The people that take part in the counts vary widely as to their ability to identify birds, ranging from those birders that are members of the elite 700 Club (birders that have spotted and identified at least 700 species of birds in North America) to beginners armed with nothing more than a pair of binoculars, a field guide, and a desire to learn.

While Christmas Bird Counts serve an important conservation purpose, they are also lots of fun, educational, a competitive sporting event, and a social activity. Beginning birders are given the opportunity to hone their birding skills with the help of experienced birders, who willingly share invaluable bird-identification tips. For someone starting out or simply trying to become a better birder, time spent with an expert is invaluable.

Count teams work hard to see if they can see more birds than last year's squad or to set new count records for various species. This requires having a strategy and sticking to it. To see the greatest variety of birds, teams must visit as many different types of habitats as possible.

Counts also provide wonderful opportunities for people to renew old acquaintances as well as forge new ones. Good cheer abounds as team members swap stories and celebrate the sighting of each new species, and spirits soar when a species is discovered that has never been reported in previous counts.

If you go on this count, you will have the opportunity to see the fascinating birdlife that inhabits the Georgia mountains in winter. Typically, fifty or more species are seen on a count. Some of the birds seen on recent counts

Spotting an evening grosbeak on a Christmas Bird Count is always a special event.

include red-breasted and white-breasted nuthatch, brown creeper, tufted titmouse, Carolina chickadee, golden-crowned and ruby crowned kinglet, hermit thrush, fox sparrow, white-crowned sparrow, and red crossbill, to name a few.

If leisurely hiking through the mountains on a crisp, early winter day with really nice people appeals to you, don't miss this count. Anyone interested in embarking on this adventure should call ahead to make sure that the count date and starting time have not changed. Participants traditionally meet at the Chatsworth Office of the U.S. Forest Service at 8:00 A.M. on count day.

Food and lodging: At least fifteen restaurants and one motel are located within 5 miles of the U.S. Forest Service Office.

For more information:
U.S. Forest Service
Cohutta Ranger District
401 Old Ellijay Road
Chatsworth, GA 30705
(706) 695–6737

Georgia Nongame-Endangered Wildlife Program
116 Rum Creek Drive
Forsyth, GA 31029
(478) 994–1438

The Georgia Ornithological Society Web site: www.gos.org

45

Wings Over the Swamp Wildlife Festival

The Okefenokee Swamp has been home to sandhill cranes for thousands of years. This festival celebrates this timeless relationship.

Recommended time: 7:00 A.M. to 4:00 P.M. during the second weekend in February.

Name and location of site: Okefenokee National Wildlife Refuge, approximately 12 miles from Folkston.

Minimum time commitment: Six hours.

What to bring: Camera, binoculars, field guide to birds.

Admission fee: $5.00 per car.

Directions: From Folkston, at the junction of SR 40 and SR 121, turn onto SR 121 and travel south 8 miles to the junction of the Okefenokee Parkway. Turn right (west) on the Okefenokee Parkway. The visitors center is in another 4.3 miles, at the end of the Okefenokee Parkway.

The background: The Okefenokee National Wildlife Refuge occupies much (395,080 acres) of the Okefenokee Swamp, which is in southeastern Georgia and hugs the Georgia-Florida border.

There are three entrances to the swamp: through Stephen Foster State Park, along the swamp's western border; through Okefenokee Swamp Park, the northern entrance; and through the Suwannee Canal Recreation Area, the refuge's main entrance, where the annual Wings Over the Swamp Wildlife Festival is held during Sandhill Crane Awareness Week in February.

The refuge is a complex of six different habitat types, including more than seventy islands, shrub swamp, blackgum forests, open water, and prairies. The marshy prairies are perhaps the best known habitats in the swamp, where floating islands, often called trembling earth, are found. These islands are formed when mats of decaying vegetation are forced to the surface of the water by methane and other gases, and they are up to a foot thick and can sometimes support the weight of a person.

With such habitat diversity, it is not surprising that the swamp is home to a vast array of fascinating plants and animals, including 234 species of birds, otters, black bears, alligators, white-tailed deer, turtles, snakes (such as the threatened indigo), fish, and amphibians. Some of the plants that grow here are red root, bladderwort, pitcher plant, and golden club.

A visitors center, six walking trails, an observation tower, and boat and canoe trails offer visitors great opportunities to become acquainted with the plants and animals that make the Okefenokee, commonly called The Land of Trembling Earth (for the floating islands in the swamp that move when you walk on them), a must-see for wildlife enthusiasts.

The fun: If you are looking for a fun-filled day at one of the premiere watchable-wildlife destinations in the Southeast, the Wings Over the Swamp Wildlife Festival has something for everyone. The stars of the show are sandhill cranes, and the Okefenokee is the year-round home of the Florida sandhill crane and the winter home of the greater sandhill crane. The cranes can be seen from the 0.75-mile long boardwalk and 50-foot observation tower at Chesser Prairie or on a canoe or boat trip into the swamp. Boats, motors, and canoes can be rented from a private concessionaire. Guided boat tours are also available.

Although cranes are the center of attention, the festival also celebrates the other birds that make their homes in the swamp. Special events include live birds of prey shows, workshops, children's activities, seminars, and field trips.

If you want to spend some time away from the festival's organized activities, take a drive down the wildlife drive or walk one of the refuge's nature trails. The paved wildlife drive winds its way through the forest that covers the uplands at this end of the swamp. Small parking areas are provided at prime viewing sites. Keep your eyes peeled for raccoons, fox squirrels, deer, armadillos, endangered red-cockaded woodpeckers, and other birds. If you only have time to walk one trail, choose the Swamp Walk Trail, which leads to the Owl Roost Tower in Chesser Prairie. There is much to see on this trail, so don't leave your camera in the car.

Most visitors to the Okefenokee want to see alligators, but whether you will see one depends on how cold it is. Gators won't be seen if temperatures dip. On bright sunny days, gators are often seen from the boardwalk at Chesser Prairie.

One of the most common birds that you will encounter along the trail is the yellow-rumped warbler. Formerly known as the myrtle warbler, this small songster, true to its new name, has a conspicuous yellow rump. The bird will be seen gleaning small insects from the branches of trees and shrubs along the trail.

Look for wading birds and waterfowl in the prairie. Wood and ring-necked ducks are seen in the swamp during the winter. Great blue heron, great egret, and white ibis can also be spotted here.

At the end of the trail, your climb to the top of Owl Roost Tower will be rewarded with a bird's-eye view of the swamp. Look carefully for flocks of the long-necked and long-billed sandhill cranes, which are gray and have tails that look like full bustles.

If you happen to hear calling off in the distance that sounds like the baying of hounds, sandhill cranes may be winging their way toward Chesser Prairie. The sight and sound of sandhill cranes descending into the marshy prairie in front of you would be a thrilling experience for even the most well-traveled wildlife-watcher. As the birds get closer, their loud honking becomes almost musical, and it has been described as sounding something like *Ah-honk, Ka-ronk, Ka-lunk*. Sandhills, like other cranes, fly with their necks out and legs extended well beyond their tails. If they come into sight, watch as their wings take a slow downstroke and rapid upstroke.

When you see or hear sandhill cranes in the Okefenokee Swamp, you are witnessing a natural spectacle that has been taking place for thousands of years. While the world has undergone unbelievable changes during the time that cranes have been residents of the swamp, it is comforting to know that some things like sandhill cranes remain timeless.

Food and lodging: More than a dozen restaurants, four motels, and four campgrounds are in Folkston and in the surrounding area within 15 miles from the site.

For more information:
Refuge Manager
Okefenokee National Wildlife Refuge
Route 2, Box 3330

Folkston, GA 31537

(912) 496–7836

For information regarding boat and canoe rentals, contact:

Suwannee Canal Recreation Concession, Inc.

Route 2, Box 3325

Folkston, GA 31537

(912) 496–7156 or (800) SWAMP96

46

In Search of the Purple Sandpiper

The combination of abundant birdlife, uncrowded beaches, and pleasant temperatures make the beginning of the year a great time to be outdoors on Tybee Island.

Recommended time: January and February.

Name and location of site: The North Beach of Tybee Island, less than 20 miles from Savannah. (See map on page 59.)

Minimum time commitment: One to two hours.

What to bring: Binoculars, spotting scope, field guide to birds, sunscreen.

Admission fee: The parking fee at North Beach Parking Lot is 25 cents per fifteen minutes or $6.00 a day.

Directions: From Savannah, at the junction of I–16 (exit 165) and SR 204, take SR 204 and go 1.5 miles to US 80. Turn left on US 80 and continue east 16.4 miles to Campbell Road on Tybee Island. Turn left on Campbell Road, travel 0.2 mile, and turn left onto Van Horne Street. Continue 0.1 mile and turn right onto Meddin Drive. Travel 0.4 mile to the North Beach Parking Lot, which is located behind the Tybee Museum.

The background: Tybee Island, the northernmost island along the Georgia coast, is quite young geologically speaking. While other nearby islands are some 40,000 years old, Tybee was formed only 1,000 years ago.

Located at the mouth of the Savannah River, this small island, measuring only 2.5 miles long and less than a mile wide, was originally inhabited by the Euchee Indians. These Native Americans named the island "tybee," which means salt in their language. Today the island is home to approximately 4,000 year-round residents, and it is also a popular destination for tourists who flock here to enjoy the natural beauty and laid-back atmosphere.

The fun: Most people think of visiting the Georgia coast only in the summer. While summer is indeed a great time to enjoy the sights and sounds of this vacation Mecca, those that limit their visits to the summer miss the opportunity to see the coast at times when many feel it is most beautiful.

In winter, shorebirds outnumber beachcombers by a wide margin at Tybee Island. While the semipalmated plovers, ruddy turnstones, willets, sanderlings, and dunlins here can be seen on any of the other islands along the Georgia coast, Tybee Island is *the* place to see the purple sandpiper. Most years, this rare Georgia visitor is seen nowhere else in the Peach State.

The name "purple sandpiper" conjures up the image of a grape-colored bird that might be seen on Sesame Street. Actually, it was named for the faint purplish gloss of its back and wings that can occasionally be seen at very close range.

The purple sandpiper is a dark, chunky, 7.25- to 8.25-inch-tall bird. The bird's belly is white, as is the chin of the adult. The bases of its bill and legs vary in color from dull yellow to orange. If you are able to get a very good view of the bird, you will see a white spot before its eye.

The best time to see purple sandpipers is at or near high tide. Since the arrival of high tide changes daily, consult a tide table for this area of the Georgia coast when planning your adventure.

At the end of the boardwalk that leads from the parking lot to the beach, turn left and begin walking toward the north end of the island. Look for purple sandpipers darting among the rocks of the jetties that project from the beach out into the ocean, where they feed on small crustaceans, insects, mollusks, and worms. Since the birds' dark plumage camouflages them well among the dark rocks of the jetties, carefully scan each rock before moving on.

When the tide reaches its peak, the birds will leave their rocky feeding areas and roost on the beach. At this time, look for purple sandpipers roosting in small groups near piles of seaweed along the shore. Often the sandpipers are seen roosting and feeding in the company of ruddy turnstones.

As you walk the beach at high tide, you will see large flocks of birds resting on the sand. Feeding areas used by many birds are flooded at high tide, and this offers the wildlife-watcher a great opportunity to closely observe birds that otherwise might be difficult to see and approach. If you are lucky, you might see black skimmers, terns, American oystercatchers, ring-billed

Purple sandpipers are often seen feeding on the wave-swept rocks along the beach.

gulls, herring gulls, piping plovers, and a host of others. When you approach a resting flock, give it a wide berth. If flocks of birds are constantly flushed by people strolling the beach, they use up valuable energy reserves and may even abandon the beach entirely.

Scan the offshore waters as you walk along the beach. Besides the brown pelicans and gulls that are commonly seen feeding along the beach, be on the lookout for large white birds with black wingtips, which are Northern gannets. These distinctive birds are known for their spectacular diagonal dives into the water from heights of up to 100 feet. Northern gannets rarely come to shore, preferring instead to feed some 300 miles from shore.

If you like beachcombing for shells, the north end of Tybee is considered the best place to shell on the entire island.

Food and lodging: Numerous restaurants and motels are on the Island.

For more information:
Tybee Island Information Center
P.O. Box 491
Tybee Island, GA 31328
(912) 786–5444

47

Winter

Butterflies Galore

*The splendor of more than 1,000 free-flying tropical butterflies
swirls around you as you walk through the nation's largest butterfly
conservatory.*

Recommended time: Winter.

Name and location of site: Cecil B. Day Butterfly Center, just outside
of Pine Mountain.

Minimum time commitment: One to two hours.

What to bring: Camera and lots of film.

Admission fee: One-day adult admission $12; one-day child (ages six to
twelve) admission $6.00.

Directions: In Pine Mountain, at the junction of SR 354 and US 27, turn
right onto SR 354 and continue east approximately 0.5 mile to the entrance
of Callaway Gardens, on the left.

The background: The Cecil B. Day Butterfly Center is located at
Callaway Gardens, a 2,500-acre garden and recreation area operated by the
nonprofit Ida Cason Callaway Foundation. Since its opening in 1988, the
Cecil B. Day Butterfly Center has earned the reputation of being one of the
finest butterfly conservatories in the world.

Visitors to this, the largest glass-enclosed tropical butterfly conservatory in
North America, have the unique experience of walking among more than
1,000 free-flying butterflies representing fifty to eighty species. The butterflies
on display at the center are native to Africa, Taiwan, and Malaysia, as well as
Central and South America.

A popular feature at the center is the one-and-a-half-acre butterfly garden planted around the center. Here, visitors can observe native butterflies and learn what plants can be used to attract these flying jewels to their own backyards.

The fun: From the minute you enter the Cecil B. Day Butterfly Center, you are surrounded by butterflies. Butterfly pictures adorn the walls and carpets, the gift shop specializes in butterfly-related gift items, and maps, complete with mounted butterflies, illustrate the diversity and distribution of butterflies throughout the world. The center's theater shows a colorful and informative film, *On Wings of Wonder,* which details the life of the butterfly.

While the film and displays get you thinking about butterflies, nothing can properly prepare you for the sight that awaits you when you open the door and walk into the conservatory. Immediately you are surrounded with countless butterflies amid the beauty of a garden of tropical plants. Butterflies fill the air, sipping nectar from tropical blooms and butterfly feeders, while others perch on vegetation inches from your head. As soon as you focus your attention on one butterfly, someone in your party will be anxiously calling for you to look at another.

Your first impulse will be to continue walking along the winding path, seeking butterflies that are bigger or prettier than those you have already seen. If you do this, you'll reach the exit having seen only a fraction of the butterflies living in the conservatory. Not to worry; you can always reenter the conservatory and take more time the second time around.

It is common for butterflies to alight on you as you walk through the facility. If this happens, don't become alarmed or roughly swat these tame insects. Without touching the wings of the fragile animal, gently coax it to a nearby leaf or flower.

With butterflies fluttering about everywhere, overlooking the hatching boxes is easy. Take the time to check them out. They house the chrysalises of butterflies that will eventually be released into the conservatory. The chrysalises of many species are just as colorful as the adult butterflies themselves, and some even appear to be made of gold.

While the butterflies are the stars of the show, the conservatory also houses a small collection of waterfowl and hummingbirds. In fact, some of the hummingbirds living in the facility have even nested here. Hummingbirds are difficult to find, so don't be surprised if you don't spot them.

Since butterfly-watching and gardening are rapidly growing in popularity, one highlight of any trip to the butterfly center is a stroll around the butterfly gardens planted next to the conservatory. Perhaps the best time to visit this feature is in September, when the diversity and numbers of our native butterfly species are high.

This garden is also a great demonstration garden where you can observe the colors, foliage, and growth characteristics of plants that you might consider adding to your own home landscape. Be sure to bring plenty of film—with photographic opportunities everywhere, this is the last place you want to run out of film.

Food and lodging: More than two dozen restaurants, eleven hotels, four bed-and-breakfasts, and two campgrounds are within 5 miles of the butterfly center.

For more information:
Education Department
Callaway Gardens
P.O. Box 2000
Pine Mountain, GA 31822-2000
(800) 663–5101

48

Winter

A Glimpse at the Secret Life of an Owl

Owling at dusk often requires exceptional listening and viewing skills. Short-eared owls make it a bit easier as they are known to hunt in daylight.

Recommended time: December through February.

Name and location of site: Cobb (town), 16.1 miles (twenty-two minutes) west of Cordele.

Minimum time commitment: One to two hours.

What to bring: Binoculars, field guide to birds.

Admission fee: None.

Directions: From Cobb, at the junction of US 280 and Cobb Cheek Road (CR 18), turn right on Cobb Cheek Road and continue 1.5 miles to the junction of Tim Tucker Road. From here you can either turn left onto Tim Tucker Road and begin looking for the owls in the fields to the right of the road or continue on, scanning the fields to the left of the road.

The background: Owls are widely believed to be strictly denizens of the night. While it is true that most owls hunt almost exclusively at night, a few species hunt both day and night, including the short-eared owl. Whenever you can find the haunts of the short-eared owl, you have a front-row seat to one of nature's most exciting and seldom seen dramas—an owl hunting its prey.

The vast agricultural lands around the tiny town of Cobb are recognized as one of the chief wintering habitats of this northern migrant in the Peach

State. Here, a quiltlike pattern of cultivated fields interspersed with small wet-lands and brushy field borders offer wintering short-eared owls an abundance of roosting habitat and prey.

The short-eared owl is a medium-size owl, roughly the size of a crow (15.5 inches long). It is light brown in color with a distinctive pale patch on the upper wing and a long dark area on the underside of the wing near the wrist. A marking that resembles sunglasses surrounds its eyes.

The bird was named for the small earlike tufts of feathers that protrude from the top of its head. You will be extremely lucky to see the "ears" as they most often lie flat against the head.

Short-eared owls range widely throughout the world, Australia being the only continent where they are absent. In North America, they nest through-out Canada and Alaska southward to a line extending from northern Arizona to Missouri, Pennsylvania, and New Jersey. The birds winter across much of the contiguous United States and into Mexico.

The fun: Short-eared owls normally begin feeding at dusk after spending their days sleeping on the ground in thick vegetation. However, since they sometimes feed during the day, beginning your search for the owl during the late afternoon is best. This will give you plenty of time to find habitats that the owl prefers and will also give you the chance to see one or more of the birds hunting in bright sunlight. If you are lucky enough to see a short-eared owl abroad at this time of day, don't be surprised if it harasses a passing crow or great blue heron. They have even been known to harry flocks of vultures.

Look for patches of thick grass and brush alongside fields. Dense patches near fields that have been harvested, leaving rows of stubble, are particularly good places to watch for owls as they offer the owls places to feed close by roosting sites.

While it is possible to see the owls perched near a field, more than likely the birds will be spotted in flight. When hunting, they fly a few feet above the ground searching for prey. Their wingbeat is best described as floppy. When they spot a vole or other prey, they will sometimes hover mothlike for thirty seconds, listening and watching before dropping, feet extended, on the hapless animal. Occasionally they will sit on their victims; more frequently, however, they grab their prey without ever landing on the ground. Their catch is then carried to a nearby perch and eaten.

The only bird that you might mistake a short-eared owl for is a northern harrier. Northern harriers also patrol fields in a similar manner; however, they look quite different. Besides the owl's distinctive markings, in flight it will appear to have a round, neckless head. In comparison, northern harriers are larger (17 to 23 inches long) and appear much slimmer. Both male and female northern harriers have distinctive white patches at the bases of their tails. Adult males are grayish above and light-colored below, and their wingtips are black. Females and immatures have brownish heads, necks, backs, and tails and streaked breasts.

Since northern harriers feed exclusively during the day, as the day fades into night they will cease feeding and roost. Because they also roost on the ground, it is easy to mistake a harrier fluttering down to its roosting site at dusk for a short-eared owl.

Most short-eared owls are seen in poor light. Since they fly so close to the ground, they are often difficult to see against the brownish ground cover. At times you may be lucky enough to spot a bird flying out over a bright green field or wheat or other grain crop. If you are very still and a hunting bird passes close by, listen for soft musical cooing. This sound is only made by birds hunting alone.

While the short-eared owl's show is truly spectacular, it is much too short. Soon after they begin flying, darkness will blanket the south Georgia countryside, leaving you wanting to return for another performance.

Food and lodging: More than a dozen restaurants are between I–75 and the viewing site. In addition, travelers have their choice of more than six motels in Cordele. At the nearby Georgia Veterans State Park, there are seventy-seven tent, trailer, and RV sites and ten cottages.

For more information:
Georgia Nongame-Endangered Wildlife Program
116 Rum Creek Drive
Forsyth, GA 31029
(478) 994–1438

49

Winter

The Gray Squirrel's Country Cousin

The longleaf pine–wiregrass ecosystem of southern Georgia is a favored haunt of the fox squirrel.

Recommended time: Late November through December.

Name and location of site: Seminole State Park, approximately 20 miles from Bainbridge.

Minimum time commitment: Two hours.

What to bring: Binoculars, camera.

Admission fee: Daily parking is $2.00 per vehicle; an annual Georgia ParkPass is $25. Discounts are available for senior citizens.

Directions: From just northwest of Bainbridge, at the intersection of US 27 and SR 253, turn west onto SR 253 and drive 20.1 miles to the park on the left.

The background: The fox squirrel ranges throughout the state of Georgia, preferring to live in mature hardwood or longleaf pine forests. Nowhere, however, is this large squirrel more abundant than in the longleaf pine–wiregrass habitats in the southern part of the state.

Wildlife biologists estimate that fox squirrel populations have declined some 85 percent since the arrival of the first European settlers in the Southeast. This is due in large part to the destruction of longleaf pine–wiregrass habitats. Today only 3 percent of this rich ecosystem remains.

Seminole State Park's open longleaf pine woodlands are ideally suited to this fascinating mammal. Regular, prescribed burns keep the forest floor

Fox squirrels are often seen in the park's picnic areas.

open, which benefit the fox squirrel since it spends much of its day foraging for food on the ground.

The fun: December is an ideal time to visit Seminole State Park in search of the fox squirrel. The weather is pleasant, and biting and stinging insects are rarely a problem. In addition, fox squirrels are far easier to see at that time than they are during the late spring and summer. When temperatures soar into the 90s and above, fox squirrels spend most of the day tucked away in tree cavities or leaf nests. At this time of year, fox squirrels are most active early or late in the day. In comparison, in late fall and winter, you are likely to spot a fox squirrel anytime during the day.

One of the easiest ways to spot a fox squirrel is by simply driving slowly through the park. While they can be seen practically anywhere in the park, three of the best places are on both sides of the road near the cottages as well as in the camping area. More than likely you will see the squirrels feeding on the ground either on acorns or longleaf pine seeds. You may even be lucky enough to see a fox squirrel burying acorns.

It is fun to search for fox squirrels while hiking through the park. You can either hike along the park roads or take off cross country along the park's nature trail, which is more than 2 miles long and meanders through an excellent example of endangered longleaf pine–wiregrass habitat.

As you walk along, keep a sharp eye out for telltale clues that fox squirrels have passed that way, including torn up longleaf pinecones. Fox squirrels will tear apart the cones to reach the nutritious seeds they contain. When fox squirrels are present, the remains of several pinecones will often be present in a small area.

Fox squirrels use both tree cavities and leaf nests as dens; scan the trees for both. Fox squirrels can sometimes be seen peeping their heads out of tree cavities. At first glance, leaf nests will look like large bird nests, but upon closer examination you will notice that fox squirrel nests are not flat on top, instead being large balls of leaves and other debris sitting high in a tree. Fox squirrels construct these nests from Spanish moss, twigs, grass, and leaves.

Once you spot a fox squirrel, try to discover what it is doing. More than likely it will be feeding. If so, try to figure out what it is eating. Besides pine seeds and acorns, fox squirrels also dine on berries, corn, leaves, bark, buds, plants, and fungi.

If you happen upon some squirrel bones during your explorations, you can tell whether they belonged to a fox or gray squirrel. The first thing to look at is the color of the bones: Gray squirrels have white bones, while fox squirrel bones are pink. Next look at the skull: Gray squirrels have twenty-two teeth compared to the fox squirrel's twenty since gray squirrels have two more premolars in their upper jaw.

If you are lucky enough to see several fox squirrels on your visit, make note of their color patterns. No two fox squirrels seem to look the same. In fact, each animal's distinctively colored coat can be used for identification. Some fox squirrels appear to be almost solid black, while others have black splotches. Typically, the fox squirrels in the park are grayish with varying amounts of black, and their ears and noses are usually white.

After you have spent a quiet afternoon trying to track down Georgia's largest squirrel among the towering, wide-spaced longleaf pines on the shores of Lake Seminole, you will see why many feel these fox squirrels live in one of the most beautiful spots in Georgia.

Food and lodging: At least five motels and fourteen restaurants are within 20 miles of the park. In addition, there are ten cottages and fifty tent, trailer, and RV sites in the park.

For more information:
Seminole State Park
Route 2
Donalsonville, GA 31745
(229) 861–3137

The City Squirrel and the Country Squirrel

On your trip to Seminole State Park, you are likely to see both fox and gray squirrels. Although they may seem similar, they are actually quite different.

The gray squirrel is the squirrel that we spot most often in city parks and backyards. Statewide, gray squirrels outnumber fox squirrels by a large margin. However, at Seminole they are far less common than fox squirrels. The reason for this is simple: Fox squirrels prefer the open, mature longleaf pine forests that predominate in this state park, while gray squirrels prefer forests with mature oaks, hickories, and other hardwoods.

Fox squirrels also spend more time on the ground than their uptown relatives. Seminole State Park's open camping areas and adjacent longleaf pine forest allow these intriguing mammals to easily scamper across the ground in search of food. If you happen across a fox squirrel, don't waste your time trying to run it down. While it will often run some distance before climbing up a tree to safety, it will easily outdistance you; they can run 10 to 12 miles per hour when trying to avoid an enemy. Gray squirrels, on the other hand, usually beeline to the nearest tree to escape danger.

Most gray squirrels look like they were turned out on an assembly line: All have light gray coats. In comparison, every fox squirrel seems to don a different pattern of white, gray, black, and reddish hair. If you only see fox squirrels in the South, you probably wonder where the fox squirrel got its name. Southern fox squirrels are usually predominantly black, while those in the Northeast are normally grayish. You will have to travel farther west to see fox squirrels wearing coats that are similar in color to those of their namesake, the red fox.

The most obvious difference between gray and fox squirrels is their size. Gray squirrels that hail from the Peach State rarely measure more than 17 inches long and weigh a hair more than a pound. Fox squirrels are quite a bit larger, tipping the scales at one and a half to three pounds and measuring up to 28 inches long.

Fox squirrels have home ranges that can be as small as ten acres in size, although many live in an area encompassing seventy-four acres or more. However, if food is abundant, they will rarely venture more than 200 yards from their dens.

50

Winter

Wood Ducks at Twilight

This waterfowl impoundment makes for a welcoming winter wood-duck roost.

Recommended time: January or February.

Name and location of site: Rum Creek Wildlife Management Area, in Forsyth. (See map on page 97.)

Minimum time commitment: One to two hours in the evening.

What to bring: Binoculars, flashlights, and folding chairs.

Admission fee: None.

Directions: From Forsyth, at the junction of I–75 (exit 186) and Juliette Road, travel east 4 miles on Juliette Road to the Rum Creek Wildlife Management Area.

The background: The wood-duck roost is located in a twenty-five-acre waterfowl impoundment that has the distinction of being the first Matching Aid to Restore States Habitat (M.A.R.S.H.) site in the state of Georgia. The project is part of the Ducks Unlimited national program to enhance waterfowl habitat in the United States. The impoundment is designed to provide migratory waterfowl with a place to rest and feed. The successful wintering area combines an agricultural field with a green tree reservoir, which is a place where trees are flooded in the winter and drained before leaves erupt in the spring.

In late fall, the impoundment is flooded with water pumped from Rum Creek, which allows ducks to swim and feed among the flooded trees and

The call of the hen wood duck is much louder than that of the drake.

crops freely. Without the flooding, waterfowl use of this area would be low. In late winter, the impoundment is drained, permitting the cultivation of a new food crop and preventing the death of the trees and shrubs.

The fun: Plan to arrive at the pond forty-five minutes before sunset (earlier if the day is cloudy because the ducks roost earlier in overcast weather). This will give you plenty of time to walk to the viewing area before the ducks arrive. It will take approximately ten minutes to walk from your car to the best place to watch the spectacle.

Park across the road from the metal gate that barricades the road leading to the pond. Cross Juliette Road, watching carefully for traffic, walk around the gate, and continue down the road. The M.A.R.S.H. pond will be on your left. Watch and listen for ducks swimming among the standing trees, and then follow the road onto the dike and walk about 100 yards down to where a road angles off to the left. This road leads to a grassy mound and a viewing platform, a good vantage point from which to watch the ducks flock to their roost.

As you approach the road junction, you will see a field of flooded corn. Chances are good that you will flush flocks of waterfowl that have come to feed on the grain. You may see ring-necked duck, northern shoveler, American wigeon, gadwall, American coot, mallard, black duck, and green-winged teal, to name a few.

Walk to the top of the observation platform. While you can watch for ducks from here, you will get a closer look if you position yourself along the tree/shrub line at the far side of the mound. Settle in and begin listening and watching. On most evenings a cacophony of whistles and quacks will let you know that many ducks are already present at the roost. Often birds that have been feeding on the flooded corn will simply swim into the timber to spend the night.

Occasionally, the ducks' calling will be interrupted by a loud, resounding splash that sounds much like a canoe paddle being slapped against the surface of the water. This is the sound of a beaver striking its broad, flat tail against the dark surface of the pond, which it does when it becomes alarmed.

Identifying wood ducks in the fading evening light is not as difficult as it might seem. In flight, wood ducks appear to have long tails and short, broad wings. However, unlike most ducks, when woodies are in flight they hold their heads above their bodies. Invariably, their bills will be pointing downward. If you look closely, you will even see them moving their heads up and down.

The wood duck's distinctive calls will also help you to identify the ducks silhouetted against the horizon. The male wood duck's call is a high whistled *twee, twee*, which is somewhat like the call of the American goldfinch. The female's call, a plaintive *wee-e-e-e-k, wee-e-e-e-k,* is much louder and can be heard from a considerable distance.

The woodies arrive in small flocks and will avoid the standing corn, preferring instead the security offered by the flooded timber. Many birds will zip over your head at an elevation of 20 to 30 feet or less. As the swift-flying ducks approach the timber, they display twists and turns that would be the envy of a fighter pilot. In spite of these aerial acrobatics, from time to time you will hear birds crash into branches.

During the peak of the roost flight, birds will fill the skies. Then, just as suddenly as the birds appeared, the flight is over. From far out in the timber, the calls of ducks will be heard as they seemingly jostle for position within the crowded roost.

There are several different kinds of wildlife that can be found in and around the impoundment at night, including the American woodcock. This game bird uses its long straight bill to probe for earthworms in the moist soils

North America's Most Attractive Success Story

The wood duck holds the reputation of being the most beautiful species of waterfowl in North America. Anyone fortunate enough to see a drake wood duck regaled in his iridescent green, blue, purple, and chestnut plumage would agree that this gorgeous bird is truly deserving of this honor.

At the turn of the twentieth century the wood duck ventured precariously close to the brink of extinction. Fortunately, efforts to restore wood duck populations stand as one of the most successful stories in the annals of wildlife management.

Today, while the wood duck is the most common species of waterfowl nesting in Georgia, most outdoor enthusiasts rarely see it. This is due in large part to the fact that throughout much of the year wood ducks spend their time in small groups in secluded beaver ponds, wood-lined creeks, and wooded wetlands far from the eyes of humans. However, as summer wanes, these beautiful birds begin to gather in increasing numbers at nighttime roost sites. Here the birds find protection in numbers as it is far more difficult for a predator to approach a flock of ducks within striking distance than it is a single bird. At first these nocturnal gatherings consist mainly of adult males that only have recently regained their ability to fly. In time, the drakes are joined by hens that have completed their brood-rearing chores and their now-flying young. These flocks are typically small, numbering only a dozen or two. Throughout the remainder of the summer the flocks begin to grow, and by fall and winter they can swell to more than a thousand birds.

Roost flights begin shortly after the sun has set and continue until the last vestiges of sunlight have disappeared from the western horizon. The birds begin to trickle into the roost site, and the sunlight grows dimmer. However, in a matter of minutes the flights reach a crescendo as birds that have been feeding miles from the roost site arrive. Then, just as suddenly as the flight began, it is over. The end of the flight is so abrupt that it is as if someone turned off a spigot.

The birds spend the night in small patches of open water surrounded by trees and shrubs. At dawn, the birds leave the roost to spend their day foraging for acorns, smartweed, and other favored foods.

of the bottomlands next to the M.A.R.S.H. pond and arrives at these feeding areas about a half hour after sunset. They announce their arrival with a call that can be best described as a nasal *peeent,* accompanied by a twittering sound that is created by its wings.

Owls also inhabit the site, and with luck you will hear the calls of three species of owls during your visit. The tiny screech owl's call sounds like a high-pitched, mournful whistle that rises and falls in pitch. The barred owl, on the other hand, seems to be asking, *Who cooks for you, who cooks for y'all.* The great horned owl's call is muted and sounds like *hoo hoo hoooo, hoo hoo.*

When you leave the roost, try to be as quiet as possible. When ducks are disturbed at a roost site, they are reluctant to return.

Food and lodging: More than two dozen restaurants, eleven motels, and a campground are within 10 miles of the site.

For more information:
Georgia Nongame-Endangered Wildlife Program
116 Rum Creek Drive
Forsyth, GA 31029
(478) 994–1438
or
Rum Creek Wildlife Management Area
116 Rum Creek Drive
Forsyth, GA 31029
(478) 994–2439

51

Winter

Watching Dolphins on Beach Patrol

Bottlenose dolphins are easy to spot year-round from this island beach.

Recommended time: December through February.

Name and location of site: Tybee Island, approximately 18 miles east of Savannah. (See map on page 59.)

Minimum time commitment: One to two hours.

What to bring: Binoculars, spotting scope, sunscreen.

Admission fee: Parking places along the beach are metered, with fees of $1.00 per hour. The city parking lots at North Beach and Fourteenth and Sixteenth Streets cost $6.00 per day.

Directions: From Savannah, at the junction of I–16 (exit 165) and SR 204, hop on SR 204 and go 1.5 miles to US 80. Turn left on US 80 and continue 18 miles east to Tybee Island.

The background: Dolphin-watching is growing in popularity along the Georgia Coast and throughout the world. The bottlenose dolphin is the most highly visible marine mammal found in the Peach State's coastal waters, inhabiting the waters near beaches as well as bays and estuaries.

Dolphins can be seen along the coast throughout the year. While their numbers increase during the summer months, some dolphin-watchers prefer to observe them along the shore in the winter when the beaches are less crowded.

Bottlenose dolphins typically live in social groups called pods. Pods often consist of mothers and their calves, or subadult males and females. Adult males are loners or are members of small pods made up of one or two other adult males. Usually pods are smaller near the shore than they are in deeper water. Pods often range in size from two to seven or more individuals, and at times two or more pods congregate, forming large groups. These large gatherings of dolphins are called herds.

Bottlenose dolphins are up to 12 feet long, although most average 8 to 9 feet in length. An adult bottlenose may weigh anywhere from 400 to 575 pounds, with the male of the species slightly larger than the female. These dolphins are typically dark gray on their backs and light gray on their sides, with pink to white undersides. Bottlenose dolphins have been known to live as long as thirty-seven years.

The fun: Dolphin-watching is great fun. These large, graceful animals are easy to spot and follow as they make their way through the waters along the beach. Dolphin-watching can be done from one location or as you leisurely stroll along the shore.

You can see dolphins from any location along the beach on Tybee Island. Many people like to dolphin-watch along the north and south ends of the island, where there are the greatest numbers of birds. In this way they can combine dolphin- and bird-watching.

If there is a downside to dolphin-watching, it is that we usually get only fleeting glimpses of these sleek, powerful swimmers. We most often see dolphins when they come to the surface of the water to breathe, which they do through a single blowhole located atop their heads. As a dolphin nears the surface, it opens its blowhole and exhales the used air in its lungs. Consequently, any seawater that collects around the blowhole or water vapor from the lungs often creates a "blow" that can be seen from some distance. Blows are more visible when the air is cooler, similar to the way we can see our breath on a crisp winter morning. After the used air is exhaled, the animal quickly inhales, closes its blowhole, and submerges. The entire process of exhaling and inhaling takes less than a second.

How often we see a dolphin depends on what it is doing and how deep it dives. Dolphins can dive to depths of 150 feet or more and can hold their breath for up to ten minutes, although in the shallow water off Georgia's beaches, dives rarely last that long. Although dolphins are most active when they are feeding early and late in the day, dolphins can be seen anytime. However, they are most visible when seas are calm.

Following dolphins is sometimes tricky as we don't have any idea where they are going, how long they are going to stay submerged, or how fast they are swimming. While dolphins can swim 22 miles per hour for short distances, they normally cruise along at 3 to 7 miles per hour.

Since dolphins like to ride the waves created by passing boats, they can often be spotted riding both bow and stern waves. The most spectacular sight is a dolphin jumping completely out of the water, which they occasionally do up to a height of 6 feet. This behavior is called breaching.

See if you can spot a female and her calf. As you might expect, calves are smaller than their mothers. Also, be on the lookout for dolphins chasing each other. If you are really lucky, you might even see them pitching things or carrying or tossing objects such as seaweed.

If you would like to go on a dolphin-watching boat trip, contact the Tybee Island Visitors Center/Chamber, which can give you information on tour operators and prices charged for such tours. If you take a dolphin tour, don't feed the dolphins. Dolphins that learn to associate humans with food stand a very real chance of being injured or killed.

Food and lodging: There are a wide range of restaurants and motels on Tybee Island.

For more information:
Tybee Island Visitors Center/Chamber
802 First Street, Highway 80
Tybee Island, GA 31328
(912) 786–5444
www.tybeeonline.com

52

Winter

Eagle Nesting—Southern Style

Spy a pair of bald eagles carrying out their nesting duties.

Recommended time: February through March.

Name and location of site: Champney Island Boat Ramp, less than 5 miles from Darien.

Minimum time commitment: One to two hours.

What to bring: Binoculars, spotting scope, camera, field guide to birds.

Admission fee: None.

Directions: From Darien, at the junction of SR 251 and US 17, travel south for 3.8 miles to the Champney Island Boat Ramp, which will be on the east (left) side of the highway.

The background: Winter is the best time of year to see bald eagles in Georgia, and during this time the state hosts both northern and southern bald eagles. While they look identical, northern bald eagles are slightly larger than their southern cousins. Northern bald eagles nest in summer and migrate south for the winter, but southern bald eagles nest in winter. Some young bald eagles migrate north in summer while their parents rarely migrate northward, preferring instead to abandon their nest sites and wander about until it is time to nest again.

The Georgia coast offers wildlife enthusiasts excellent opportunities to see both migrant and resident bald eagles. One of the best places to observe eagles here is at the 29,278-acre Altamaha Waterfowl Management Area, which is managed for waterfowl and other wildlife. For several years bald eagles have nested here within sight of busy US 17 and the Champney Island Boat Ramp.

The fun: On this trip you will not only have the opportunity to see a bald eagle in flight, but depending on the timing of your trip, perhaps even see eagles feeding their young.

When you arrive at the boat ramp, park your vehicle about halfway down the back side of the parking lot. The grassy strip that separates the parking lot from the marsh makes a good viewing area.

When you gaze across the fifty-five-acre impoundment, you will be looking over a sea of cutgrass. The eagle nest is located on the far side of the marsh in a large pine tree. If you look directly across the marsh with your back to the parking lot, the pine tree containing the nest is approximately twenty to thirty degrees to your right. As is the case with most eagle nests, the nest is built below the top of the tree. It will appear like a giant stack of branches suspended near the tree's trunk.

Eagles are sometimes seen standing on the nest, or if a bird is incubating eggs, you may see a white head poking out above the edge of the nest. If you don't see an eagle at the nest, scan the trees to the right and left. Eagles will sometimes perch a few hundred yards away.

If you visit this site from December to mid-January, more than likely the birds will be incubating eggs. During this time, your chances of spotting an eagle are less than they will be after the young hatch. If you make this trip in February or March, eagles are much more active around the nest. During this time both the males and females bring food to their rapidly growing young.

If you view the nest when the parents are feeding their young, it is always fun to try to identify the food they are bringing to the nest. The choice of food items runs the gamut from fish, coots, and ducks to road-killed rabbits, opossums, and raccoons. The best viewing times are early in the morning and mid- to late afternoon, when the adults are most active and hunting for food. On average, a pair of bald eagles will feed their young four to eight times a day.

As the young eagles continue to grow, they can be seen in the nest. By the end of March or April, they will appear as large as their parents. At this time they can often be seen exercising their wings while perched on the rim of the nest. Once they are about twelve weeks old, they are ready to leave the nest on their first flight.

While the nest can be viewed with 8 or 10 power binoculars, a spotting scope provides the best view. Focus the scope on the nest, and then use your binoculars to look for the adults.

If you have never seen a bald eagle in the wild, the only bird that you might confuse for a bald eagle is an osprey. Remember, adult bald eagles have white heads and tails and dark bodies. The adult osprey, on the other hand, has a white head (a dark streak runs through the eye), throat, and belly and a black tail.

Food and lodging: More than a dozen restaurants and four motels are within 5 miles of Darien.

For more information:

Georgia Nongame-Endangered Wildlife Program
116 Rum Creek Drive
Forsyth, GA 31029
(478) 994–1438

Index

About the Author

Terry Johnson has been a wildlife biologist with the Georgia Department of Natural Resources, Wildlife Resources Division for more than thirty years. Currently, he is program manager of the Nongame Wildlife/Natural Heritage Section's Nongame-Endangered Wildlife Program.

Terry has received a number of awards for his conservation efforts, including being named Wildlife Conservationist of the Year by the Georgia Wildlife Federation, the Georgia Outdoor Writers Association, and the Garden Club of Georgia. He has also been honored by Ducks Unlimited for his waterfowl conservation efforts in Georgia and was dubbed the Game Management Section's Wildlife Biologist of the Year.

A member of the Georgia Outdoor Writers Association, Terry pens a weekly column for the *Monroe County Reporter* and also contributes to *The Macon Telegraph* and the Georgia Golf Course Superintendents Association magazine, *Through the Green*. His articles have earned him more than a dozen Excellence in Craft Awards from the Georgia Outdoors Writers Association.

Terry has conducted research and management on a variety of wildlife, including waterfowl, turkey, white-tailed deer, bald eagle, peregrine falcon, quail, and songbirds. He is Georgia's only resident Master Hummingbird Bander and is active in promoting nature-based tourism in Georgia.